The Book of Relief

Passages and Exercises to Relieve Negative
Emotion and Create More Ease in The Body

By

Emily Maroutian

The Book of Relief

Passages and Exercises to Relieve Negative
Emotion and Create More Ease in The Body

By

Emily Maroutian

ISBN-13: 978-1539953319

First Printing

Printed and bound in the United States of America by Createspace, a division of Amazon.com

DISCLAIMER: This book is not intended to diagnosis or treat any mental or physical illness. It is not meant to replace therapy or medications. Always follow the advice of a physician or therapist and do not do anything that would interfere with your current treatment.

empowered by

Maroutian Entertainment
Los Angeles, California
www.maroutian.com

Transformational Books
By Emily Maroutian:

A Second Opinion:
Theories and Observations on Life and Human Behavior

The Process of "I":
An Exploration into the Intertwined Relationship between
Identity and Environment

The Energy of Emotions:
The 10 Emotional Environments and How They Shape the
World Around Us

Thirty:
A Collection of Personal Quotes, Advice, and Lessons

The Empowered Self:
Over 100 Activities and Steps For Creating An Empowered
Mind

The Reconnection Cycle:
Audio Course Transcript

The Book of Relief:
Passages and Exercises to Relieve Negative Emotion and
Create More Ease in The Body

Dedication:

For everything you have been through, are going through, or will go through. I hope this book offers you some peace.

Table of Contents:

How To Use This Book:

Anyway you choose to read or use this book is fine. You're welcome to skip the overview and only read the passages and affirmations. You're welcome to do all of the relief exercises or only do two. The only wrong way to use this book is if you use it to pressure yourself and add more stress. The purpose of the book is not to add yet one more thing you need to do in your life.

It doesn't matter if you haven't picked it up for a while. It doesn't matter if you haven't done any exercises in days, weeks, months, or ever. Nothing that you did or didn't do matters right now as you're reading these lines. All that matters is what you want to do now, today.

Don't look for that answer from a place of pressure or should. You don't *have to* do any of it. You picked this book because you want relief. Remember your desire and remember it's not an obligation. Look through the exercises. Which feels good to you? Read through some of the passages and see if it offers you inspiration or clarity on what you want to do. The purpose of the book is to bring you into a state of ease, relief, and calm. A state that will help trigger your own sense of clarity on how you want to proceed in your life.

Engaging in a creative activity offers clarity. Physical exercise offers clarity. A hot bath offers clarity. A brisk walk around the neighborhood offers clarity. Meditation offers clarity. Clarity comes when the mind and body are relaxed.

This book wasn't created to give you answers; it was created to help trigger your own. You know what's the right step for you; this book only intends to put you in a mental, emotional, and physical state that will support you in making the best decision available to you.

How you choose to use and read this book is up to you. However, if you would like some form of structure to try now or later, I'm going to offer you one: This structure is not any more right or wrong than you deciding to improvise on your own. It's all about what works for you. Structure to some brings ease because it feels like security, and for others it creates pressure and stress because it feels like lack of freedom and spontaneity.

So again, the following structure is not the right way to do it; it's just one way to do it. If it's not your way, that's okay. It's up to you on how you want to proceed.

First, read the overview so you have a better understanding of how your body responds to stress. This will help you become more aware as you're learning the signs of your body's response *to* stress and release *from* stress.

Use the passages to ease the pressure of shoulds and obligations, to move stuck thinking patterns, to let go of frustrations, and to open yourself up to clarity. They're designed to offer you momentary relief so you can enter into a state of knowing on what you would like to do next. It's a pre-action state. You can use your relief to relax more, to commit to action, or to choose non-action. Maybe the relief helps you to realize that it's simply time to let go and emotionally move on. Perhaps the relief leads you to conclude that the problem isn't really a problem at all. Only you will know.

Use the affirmations to soothe and encourage yourself. Remind yourself that you're on the correct path and that you're doing it right. There is no wrong path because at any moment you can find relief, create a state of ease, and trigger clarity. Once you are clear, you'll know what to do and where to go.

Come back to the passages and affirmations whenever you need some emotional or mental relief. Feel free to highlight or mark the ones you like the best. Use your phone to take a picture of the passages that feel the most relieving. Take it with you and read them when you need it.

Read through the relief exercises and asterisk, highlight, or circle three exercises that are simple and easy for you to do. Don't pick anything that takes you too far out of your daily routine or causes you to struggle. It's important that it's integrated easily into your life as it is now. Go with your gut instincts. You can always add more or switch them up later.

Pick a start day and begin one of the exercises. Do the second exercise on the next day and the third on the next. Work it out so you do a different exercise each day but that you at least do one a day. You're welcome to do all three in one day and then two in the next day, and so on. It's up to you on how you want to structure it. You can pick five exercises if you like, or ten. As long as you do at least one a day, it's up to you on how many you alternate with, how frequently you do it, and for how long.

As you do the exercises, acknowledge that you are engaging in them for your benefit and wellbeing. Feel your sense of control and empowerment over your wellbeing. Enjoy the exercise. Feel the relief afterward. You did it.

As you're going about your day, when you encounter some stressful situations, go to the discharge resistance exercises and do the body mindfulness and grounding exercises. This will help you discharge resistance from your body. If you can learn and memorize those techniques, you can do them anywhere: on the train, at work, in class, standing in a grocery store. They will help you release and refocus.

Soon enough, you'll develop a habit of soothing yourself. You'll find your own words and your own relief passages in your mind. The moment you feel stressed, you'll be able to ease into relief because it will feel natural to you. More natural than being stressed, chronically worrying, or getting upset. These states of mind and body have been practiced for years. To tip the scale in the other direction, you must practice habits of relief and ease.

Maybe you'll start off by having 5% of the day where you feel relief or ease. In another week, it might jump to 10%. How long it takes and how high it jumps will depend on how often you practice. Once you get to the point where more of your day is spent feeling relief, ease, and calm, rather than feeling stressed, frustrated, and worried, then the balance will tip in your favor.

It will become easier and easier the more you do it. And if you have a moment of anger or stress, remind yourself that you're working it out and it's okay if you don't get it all in one day. You know more now than you did before. You're still in the process. You feel more relief than you did before you picked up this book. Sometimes, just the act of buying or picking up this book will bring you relief. If you anticipate relief, you're likely to get it.

The purpose of this book is that soon enough, you won't need it. You'll establish habits of soothing thoughts, relieving habits, and you'll create more ease in your life. So if this book does what it's intended to do, then at one point it will no longer be useful to you. You'll move past it where you won't need to develop habits of relief and ease because you will feel relief and ease naturally. It will become your normal state of functioning.

My final advice is: do what feels right, trust your gut instincts, reach for relief no matter where you are, and take it easy. Remember that the purpose of this book is relief and ease. Use those emotions as your guide to understanding what is right for you. If it induces either feeling, go with it.

Introduction:

The body plays a powerful role in stress reduction and emotional balance. We've been taught that if we simply control our thoughts, then we can reduce stress in our bodies. To some degree, that's true, but it's only partially affective. If we also engage the body, more specifically the nervous system, then we can maintain stress relief for longer periods of time and prevent future stress-inducing episodes by building resilience.

We live in a culture of stress that reinforces itself. We automatically react to a stressful world, creating stress within our bodies and minds. It then spills out from our bodies and minds into our families and communities, recycling stress back into the world. We make our decisions from stress, we have conversations through stress, we let stress dictate our behaviors and actions.

Stress is simply the activation of the nervous system through thoughts, feelings, and sensations. It is activated to help provide a resolution to the stressor. Think of this process as turning on a car. You're not going to do that unless you're ready to take it somewhere. Once the nervous system is charged up and ready for action, it continues to trigger matching thoughts and feelings that keep that process going. Think of that as the accelerator. It keeps going until it finds a resolution or — in this car metaphor — a destination.

When you're angry with someone and your nervous system is charged up, you're going to continue to think thoughts that keep you charged up. You're going to keep that car on until you've reached your destination, until your nervous system finds a resolution.

Most of the time, it doesn't find a resolution because we end up in screaming matches that reinforce the stress and keep our systems charged up. We stay mad at other people and we hold grudges for a long time. We anticipate arguments and gossip about it to others, keeping ourselves charged even when the other person isn't around. We overuse our nervous systems, which begins to affect our bodies.

If you charge up your nervous system too often for too long you're going to run out of gas. You're going to exhaust your system, which will exhaust your overall body. Imagine if you turned on your car and left it in the driveway for hours. What if you just drove in circles without a destination or resolution? What is going to happen when you have to wake up the next morning and go to work but you don't have any more gas/energy?

Stress can deplete our systems. It can give us headaches, back aches, high blood pressure, high blood sugar, heart palpitations, inflammation, sore muscles, hormone imbalances, indigestion, excessive gas, diarrhea, shortness of breath, dizziness, and many other ailments. It's believed that 70-90% of doctor visits are related to symptoms of stress, which is mostly an over-activated nervous system.

Stress can physically alter our brain patterns and make it more difficult to see our problems in more logical ways. It can fog our brains and make simple tasks more difficult. Stress builds up the amygdala, the fear center of our brain, making us more sensitive to fear, anxiety, and worry. It can keep us charged up and "on" for no real reason. Small problems that used to pass without much emotional upset can now drain us, make us anxious, and make us ill.

The nervous system is designed to help us survive. When it is turned on, or charged up, it's ready to fight for survival. It's ready to take on danger or run away from it. It's our fight-or-flight mechanism and when stress activates it, it needs to discharge. You have to turn off the car or else you're going to run out of gas.

Have you known someone who is "on" all the time? They worry about everything, they're anxious over things they can't control, they're aggressive and pick fights with others? They can't seem to find relief or peace. Maybe that's you. Either way, that's a result of a hyperactive mind that can't seem to find resolution or ease because of habitual stress.

The hyperactive mind comes from a charged up nervous system. Its thinking pattern is: if I turn off the car, what if an emergency happens and I need to jump in it and go? I can't be "off" because it'll make me vulnerable. If I rest, if I'm happy, if I let my guard down, then something terrible will happen. So it's better to keep the car running just in case.

The great thing about the car is that as long as you put fuel in it, change its oil, and take care of its needs, it'll always turn on when you need it. You do worse to it when you leave it on, don't use it, and deplete its energy reserve.

The good news is that whatever damage stress has done to your body or mind is reversible. When we learn how to allow the stress to pass through us, how to regain calm, and how to restore ease, we can begin reversing the damage.

Ease is something we learn and cultivate through practice. Ease isn't simply having calming and relaxing thoughts. It's also equal parts feeling relief in the body. It's turning off the car when you don't need it. If your body is still charged up, it's going to be harder to maintain ease in your mind.

Your nervous system is designed to bring you ease and relief naturally if you allow it to happen without reactivating the charge. If you continue to bombard it with stress, fear, and worry, you're going to create cycles of dis-ease and imbalance both within your body and mind.

Most diseases are from chronic stress, which creates imbalances in the body. When the body can't find ease and return to regulation, it throws all your other systems off balance. Your digestive system goes haywire, your cognitive systems slow down, your sleep becomes dysregulated, you overeat or under-eat, your muscles begin to ache, your immune system weakens, and you feel fatigued. Now, you are more likely to become sick.

The Book of Relief

Ease is about feeling relief in the body and mind, which restores balance in both. This book will teach you exercises that will help you find some relief from stress, frustration, and upset. Practicing them will allow your body to cultivate ease and relief, restoring the functioning of its systems. This will not only help you become healthier, but it'll also help you make better choices in times of stress thus ensuring that you don't fall into negative cycles. Instead of reacting from a negative emotion, you will be acting from a calmer state. Your actions will be much more powerful, and they will align with your true intentions.

Negative emotions need resolution and release. Once you relieve the negative emotion, then you can choose from a state of clarity. Then, you can actively create your life as opposed to reacting to life. We rarely regret the choices we made when we were calm, clear-headed, and sure.

A negative emotion is not necessarily a bad emotion. All emotions serve a purpose in human beings. They can alert us to our internal states or inspire action to create resolution. Anger might alert us to a false sense of powerlessness or a perceived hurt. It might show us that we feel a lack of control over our current situation and are expressing anger to regain it. Sadness might show us that we are no longer happy with the circumstances of our lives and that it's time to make some of the changes we have been avoiding.

Negative emotions are guides. If we listen to what they have to say instead of acting through them, we can better our lives in a more healthy and productive way. Instead of making life choices from anger or sadness, we can choose actions that bring us relief first, which will then help us make better choices regarding those situations.

This is the cycle most people are stuck in: something happens, we feel a negative emotion about it, we react through that emotion, and we create an outcome that leaves us feeling negative. Then we repeat that over and over again.

When you have a negative emotion arise, the best course of action is to find relief first before committing any action. We usually commit an action right afterward and end up making things worse. This book will help you create the gap between negative emotion and decision. The gap will be relief.

The following pages are broken down in three parts. The first part offers information regarding the nervous system and how it handles stress. Once you understand how the nervous system works, you'll be able to become aware of when you're intentionally activating calm and relief.

The next part is full of relief passages to induce relief and allow you to let go more. It is written in *"You"* statements because receiving comforting words from others can be very soothing. It also contains a section of soothing *"I"* statements. While it's wonderful to have others offer us soothing words when we need it, it's far more powerful to offer them to ourselves. "I" statements are powerful because when you learn to ease or comfort yourself, you will do it automatically in moments of stress. They also have powerful effects on our psyche and can change the way we relate to ourselves. Now let's change the previous statement and add an "I". "I" statements are powerful because when I learn to ease and comfort myself, I will do it automatically in moments of stress.

That last statement feels much better because it places the power in your hands by making action available to you. It helps you feel the resolution even before it happens. Sometimes, that's all you really need as a resolution. Sometimes, the answer is to feel better about a situation instead of committing any physical action.

The last part of this book contains exercises that physically trigger the part of the nervous system that induces calm and relaxation. It's important to practice them as often as you can, even if you're not feeling stressed. Make calm a habit of being. They're mostly simple exercises that we do without realizing we are calming ourselves. Our bodies are smart enough to let us know what feels relieving. Make it a habit to listen and follow through.

Soothing yourself is a habit. Talking yourself down from stress or anxiety is a habit. Staying aware of how your body reacts and responds is a habit. It's something we learn and cultivate. We must practice it until we can do it automatically without conscious thought.

If we can learn anxiety and worry as automatic habits of thought, then we can learn calm and ease as well. Think of it as a reprogramming of your thought cycles. When you include the body in the reprogramming of the mind, it is much more effective because anything we experience in the body is automatically accepted as true. When your heart races, you can't ignore that. When your stomach hurts, you can't ignore that. When your foot goes numb, you can't ignore that. All experiences in the body feel true, therefore the key to lasting change is to involve the body.

This is why anxiety is so easy to learn and perpetuate, because it shows up in the body. It's a bodily experience and therefore it can't be denied. A fearful thought is accompanied by physical sensations. When we activate the body with thoughts, we program new beliefs. Not feeling safe in the moment might make us program "I'm never safe" simply because we experience the physical sensations of danger in our bodies. It *feels* true in our body and therefore we believe the experience. And because we don't want to experience it again, we make changes to our behaviors or actions to avoid recreating that feeling in our bodies.

What we try to avoid is not other people or external circumstances, but our own internal reactions. There are people who feel safe in war zones. There are people who are happy even though they live in poverty. There are people who aren't scarred by tragedy. It's not what happens to us; it's how we internalize it and how it shows up in our bodies.

As you learn to activate your body's calming mechanisms, as you feel more relief, you'll create habits and beliefs of calm and ease throughout your body and mind. You'll restore your body's natural balance, and you might even find that some of your physical symptoms disappear.

As you read the following passages or do the relief exercises, pay close attention to how your body relaxes or releases tension. Where do you feel it? Does your body become warmer? Can you feel the tight muscles in your legs ease? Do your eyes want to close? Does your breathing become slower? Stay in your body as it finds ease once again. Acknowledge the change. Notice that it's working. This will bring you more ease. It'll compound the relief you feel.

This book can offer you some soothing words when you can't find your own. It'll teach you exercises you can practice to create a habit of relief in your body. It'll teach you to discharge stress and find more balance. It'll also offer you some soothing affirmations you can repeat throughout your day. Memorize them. Repeat them. Soothe yourself over and over again. Regain your power over your experiences and reactions.

My intention for this book is that it offers relief to anyone who picks it up. I hope that includes you.

PART 1
OVERVIEW

The Automatic Nervous System:

The nervous system has many intricate components, but we're only going to focus on the automatic nervous system, which is divided in two parts: the sympathetic nervous system (the charge and activation system) and the parasympathetic nervous system (the rest and relaxation system). One is responsible for getting your mind and body ready to survive a threat and the other returns your mind and body to balance and restoration. A simple way of remembering which system does what is through the first letter. Sympathetic starts with the letter S, like stress. Parasympathetic starts with the letter P, like peace. This should help you remember which does what.

The sympathetic nervous system is the part of the system that hears the alarm bell and sets everything in motion during a threat. It floods your body with stress hormones to make sure the appropriate biological changes take place for your survival. It's the initiator of the stressful response. It changes your breathing, making it more rapid. It increases your heart rate, sharpens your senses, and slows down your digestive system to conserve energy. It makes your muscles tense and ready for action. It increases your blood pressure and blood sugar so you have more energy to survive.

The parasympathetic nervous system brings the body back into balance after a stressful elevation. It returns your heart rate back to normal, it releases the tension in your muscles, it brings your digestion back into balance. It is responsible for our body's homeostasis. When you are at ease, when you are relaxed, that's your parasympathetic nervous system at work.

A normal nervous system will complete this process and return to a balanced body. An overly activated nervous system will keep the high alert state active for longer than needed, keeping stress hormones circulating your systems and causing problems. With a hyper-alert mind it's almost as if there's no real off switch or that the off switch isn't so easy to flip because it seems to go back on without much effort. In this case, we spend more time in the arousal state than the relaxed one.

When we encounter stress, the nervous system begins a process. If it is able to complete that process, we remain healthy, resilient, and peaceful. If it can't complete the process, then we remain frustrated, stressed, angry, depressed, and anxious. Even though the initial stressor is gone, we are still left with an internal upset that doesn't find relief. This also makes us more susceptible to other stressors. This is usually what people refer to when they say they're chronically stressed or anxious.

Every time we go through the process but don't complete it, we are more susceptible to going through it again and again, lowering our resistance to stress and making it more likely to reoccur. Little problems soon feel like bigger problems, and we become overwhelmed.

The nervous system regulates your heartbeat, your breathing, your blood flow, blood pressure, body temperature, and your eating and sleeping habits. But when your nervous system becomes dysregulated, or off-balance, all of those things become more easily affected by stress. A simple comment, a long line, dirty dishes in the sink, and other small incidents will affect your body in the same way as big events would, like trauma or tragedy. Since the nervous system has become dysregulated, it no longer manages stress properly and that begins to show up in the mind and body as disorders and illnesses.

Most illnesses are a result of stress, which means that most illnesses are a result of the nervous system not fully restoring the balance in your body after a stressful event. It's likely that your nervous system activates too frequently and is over-charged for too long, causing your bodily systems to become exhausted.

The good news is that it's reversible. A simple solution to an over-stressed system is balance and restoration. Your body knows how to do that easily if you allow it to return to its calming state. Then, it will heal and rejuvenate itself.

Let's imagine for a moment that you're walking through the woods and you feel normal, there is no fear or activation. Then, all of a sudden, you hear a noise in some bushes. You freeze, trying to assess the situation. What if it's a bear? Your nervous system immediately activates. It focuses your mind to the possible threat and it triggers biological changes in your body.

The first thing that happens is your nervous system triggers the release of hormones, which begin the reactions in your body that are associated with survival as well as stress and anxiety.

Your heart rate, glucose levels, and blood flow increase, delivering more energy and oxygen to your brain and muscles. Your heart also pulls blood away from unnecessary organs and skin, delivering it where it's needed most in your ability to fight or run away. This might make you pale and begin to sweat. Your vision narrows, your hearing heightens, and certain cognitive processes slow down, enhancing others.

Your airways widen in the lungs to allow more air, which increases oxygen supply to the blood and the rest of the body. Your digestive system slows down to help conserve your body's energy. Your bladder relaxes so you can hold your urine longer. Sometimes, this has the opposite affect and some people might urinate on themselves from fear.

These biological changes can also bring up symptoms like nausea, headaches, diarrhea, gas, cramps, and dizziness. This can be from the increase in blood pressure, blood sugar, heart rate, or muscle tension. Either way, your body is now ready to fight for your life or to run away from the danger as fast as humanly possible. These biological changes have helped our ancestors survive for thousands of years.

Once the nervous system is activated and the body is charged up, it needs a successful discharge to return to balance and homeostasis. If it does not discharge the built-up energy, it will loop in the body and mind, creating chronic stress and worry. This is how a nervous system becomes dysregulated.

Discharge can happen through a safe getaway, a successful fight for your life, or immediate release. So if a bear jumped out of the bushes and you ran away successfully, your body would discharge the built-up energy and you would return to balance once you were safe again. If you decided to fight the bear and you were successful in scaring it away, the same thing would happen once you were safe again.

Let's try that scenario again. You're walking through the woods when the bushes begin to rattle and your nervous system is activated. You're ready to take off running. Then, all of a sudden, a little rabbit hops out and runs away. You feel immediate relief. There is no danger. You might even laugh from the relief. It's over and your nervous system returns to normal without fight or flight. Your parasympathetic nervous system kicked in. Your body returned to balance, and the built-up energy was immediately discharged without any required physical action.

Most of the stress we encounter in our daily lives doesn't require physical altercations or an escape. However, it's the same charged-up reaction for our bodies. The nervous system doesn't know the difference between the real bear in the bushes and your boss scolding you in an office. The threat to our wellbeing feels the same, even if your boss would never physically attack you.

A threat is registered as a threat in the body regardless of whether the threat is to our physical body/life or to our sense of self, self-esteem, beliefs, feelings, etc. Stress from a threat is registered the same. So as you begin to work on letting go and you feel more relief, your body will find more ease in daily interactions. You will be better at handling stressful situations and allowing it to pass through you instead of looping inside you. You'll begin to see the bears as rabbits.

What if you successfully escaped the bear but spent hours a day afterward thinking about what would happen if you hadn't escaped the bear? What if you replayed the incident over and over again causing your nervous system to activate and go through the same reaction even when there is no bear? This is what we do with our daily stressors. We encounter them but we don't release them mentally or emotionally. Instead, we repeat them out loud to others or we relive them in our minds over and over again, causing our bodies to relive them too. We activate ourselves by carrying our stressors in our bodies and minds.

As soon as we feel stress and are on alert from one thing, we are reminded of all the other incidents that feel the same way. This will continue to keep us in a stressful state. When we feel relief and ease, our minds think of the things that help support that state. The mind-body conversation is a loop that supports the state we're in, regardless of the state. Paranoia feeds itself, anger feeds itself, and joy feeds itself.

As your nervous system begins to release the built-up charges and lessens the frequency of activation, you will feel the difference in your body and mind. It will create a healthy loop that keeps you at ease. It doesn't take much to begin. It starts with just a little bit of relief.

The Brain-Body Conversation:

The brain and body have a conversation during an emotional experience. Contrary to what we commonly believe the body sets the tone for the experience. The brain doesn't tell the body how to react; the body tells the brain. Then, the brain either perpetuates the experience or relieves it.

If someone were to suddenly jump out at you and scare you, your body would react first long before your mind had a chance to think about what's happening. Do you stop and think, "Something is jumping out at me. I better jump back and put my hands up to defend my face"? No. You just do it automatically.

Your body speaks its own language and thinks its own thoughts. Once your brain sees that it was your friend just playing a joke, it registers the experience as non-threatening and you feel immediate relief. Your parasympathetic nervous system kicks in and your heart rate returns to normal.

In another scenario, once you see that the person who jumped out at you is a stranger trying to attack you, you run or fight. You don't think about what you should do next. You don't plan. Your body takes control and leads the way. Your thoughts about everything come later. You rationalize later. You add more to the story when telling it in retrospect. This is why people often don't know why they reacted as they did in a life-threatening situation. They often say, "I wasn't thinking." That's because they weren't thinking, not consciously. Their body was thinking for them. This is how we survive.

Our bodies hold thousands of years of ancestral survival in our muscles and DNA. Our body knows what to do to survive. It knows to fight. It knows to run. It knows to freeze. It will choose the appropriate action without your conscious decision. You will feel it in your gut long before you think it with your mind. The physiological feeling will dictate the thinking reaction. Not the other way around.

All emotions have physical symptoms. Sadness has a physical symptom. Anger has a physical symptom. Every emotion not only has matching thoughts attached to it, but also matching sensations in the body.

When you are in the physical state of tired, hungry, or cranky, your mind will produce matching thoughts. You will think about things that annoy you. You will interpret new experiences as frustrating or upsetting. Your physical state will dictate what type of thoughts come up. That's because your thinking habits are based on your physical feeling states. When you don't feel good in your body, it's hard to maintain good feeling thoughts. It can be done, but it's much more difficult. This is why it's important to create the appropriate physical atmosphere in the body first before working on the mind. Once your gut and muscles relax, then your brain can relax.

The brain and gut speak to each other through the vagus nerve. When something doesn't feel right in the gut, it triggers the appropriate reactions in the body, which then triggers matching thoughts that keep it alert.

If your body is agitated, anxious, tense, or aching, it will not send the right signals to the brain that it's okay to relax and put your guard down. If your body is on alert, it will keep your mind on alert. This is why a massage can put you to sleep but meditation can make you more anxious. Your body has to relax first before your mind can. This is how human beings are programmed. It's how we survive.

There are two methods in working with chronic stress, anxiety, and worry. The first is the traditional method of brain-to-body work. You wait until your body activates, and then you talk yourself down from it. This is what most therapy is based on; it mostly focuses on the brain's power over the body. It teaches you intellectual methods of calm and defusing.

The second method works on the body, so it doesn't activate as easily or frequently. This is known as the body-to-brain method and its highly effective for PTSD and other anxiety disorders. It brings balance and regulation to your body and increases your tolerance for stress. Both methods work for different people; however, they are better together.

One of the fastest ways of changing that brain-body conversation is to induce relief in the body. The key is to focus on the bodily symptom of the emotion as opposed to the emotion itself or the thoughts that accompany it. Let's say you feel anger and it shows up as tightness in your chest. Instead of focusing on the feeling of anger, you would focus on the symptom of tightness in your chest. That's where the anger is. Once you focus and breathe into the tightness, it will begin to release or discharge and you will feel relief.

Normally, we try to calm our symptoms with thoughts, attempting to control the body with the brain. This doesn't always work. Brain-to-body techniques can be helpful but aren't always effective because our minds have already established a habit of stressful and negative thinking that repeats itself. It doesn't take much to trigger it again.

The key is to work on both brain and body. It's important to learn how to ease negative thoughts and turn them around but it's also equally important to teach the body to release the symptoms and patterns of negative thoughts.

Body-to-brain techniques are much more powerful and effective because the body communicates to the brain that everything is now okay and the brain releases stressful thoughts thus stopping the body-brain panic/stress cycle. If you only attempt to influence the brain and body conversation through the brain, you're not going to be completely successful.

The body is designed to balance and regulate automatically. It's designed to take hit after hit and still recover and rejuvenate. Its only focus is on wellness, stability, and balance, which it maintains through discharging stress, panic, or negative emotion from an activated nervous system.

Discharge shows up in the body as trembling, sudden heat, sweating, or tingling/vibrating sensations. If you've ever had any of those symptoms show up during meditation or yoga, that's your body discharging built-up trauma, stress, or negative emotion. The reason why yoga, most of all, is effective for discharge is because the purpose of yoga is deep focus and deep breathing, which stimulates the vagus nerve. It is one of the body-to-mind methods.

However, if you don't do yoga or don't want to do yoga, that's fine too. You only require focus and breathing to influence your brain-body conversation. Some of the exercises in the last section will teach you how to do it.

The Vagus Nerve:

The vagus nerve is what makes the brain-body conversation happen. It's the telephone line connecting the conversation. It connects to the brain, heart, liver, lungs, female sex organs, pancreas, gallbladder, kidneys, gut (intestines, stomach), larynx, esophagus, ears, spleen, and tongue.

It is the longest nerve in the automatic nervous system and a pivotal component of the parasympathetic nervous system. It controls your heart rate and blood pressure. It also controls inflammation in the body, and anxiety and depression in the brain.

Your brain and gut speak to each other through this network. This is why we feel most of our anxiety, stress, or upset in our gut. We just know when something doesn't *feel* right. Our "gut reactions" to people and situations are a very real biological reaction. Since 70% of the neurons that exist outside of the brain are in the gut, it's considered to be the second brain of the body. It feels and communicates as well.

The vagus nerve plays a large role in stress relief and relaxation by releasing the neurotransmitter acetylcholine to begin the process of calming your body down after a stressful response. Its main job is to restore balance in the mind and body. Whether you were exercising, having sex, or running away from an attacker, its job remains the same: to calm you down and bring you back into normal functioning.

When your sympathetic nervous system is activated through threat or danger, it releases cortisol and adrenaline into your body to ready you for action. This activates several different biological reactions that gear you up to survive. It's the vagus nerve that returns your body back into balance by sending instructions through enzymes, proteins, and hormones, to calm those reactions. It is your body's natural anti-anxiety trigger as well as many other balancing functions.

It controls heart rate, blood pressure, digestive processes, it tells our lungs to breathe, promotes kidney function, and releases bile in the gallbladder, which helps remove toxins and break down fats. It controls glucose balance in the pancreas and liver, and it reduces inflammation all over the body. It controls taste buds in the tongue as well as saliva production. It's responsible for orgasms in women, as well as fertility. It releases tears in the eyes, helps you hold your urine, and is responsible for our feelings of compassion and empathy. It has a wide range of reach in our body and is responsible for our overall wellbeing and balance.

The reason why so much of our emotional wellbeing is tied into our body is because the vagus nerve also affects the way we feel. It doesn't just control our physical and biological reactions; it controls our emotional reactions as well.

The vagus nerve is also activated when we see images of suffering, read tragic news stories, or if we hear about an inspiring experience. It triggers our need to sympathize, to communicate with others, to feel compassion, and to bond with others. It regulates our emotional expression and is closely tied to altruism.

The stronger our vagal tone, the more compassionate, kind, and unified we feel toward others. However, when the vagal tone is weak or if the vagus nerve is under-stimulated, it's almost as if we can't "feel" for others. We lack connection and empathy. It's entirely possible that a weak vagal tone is responsible for certain psychiatric or personality disorders, including the inability to feel other people's pain.

A stronger vagal tone makes you more emotionally balanced, more optimistic, more likely to maintain longer relationships and possess better social skills and interactions. You are more likely to bounce back faster from grief, stress, suffering, or anxiety. You are also less likely to experience them in the first place. It makes you resilient and strong.

However, if the vagus nerve is over-stimulated, you might faint. It can lower your blood pressure so much that it causes you to lose consciousness. People who become queasy from the site of blood do so because the vagus nerve was over-stimulated. If you exercise so much that you want to faint, if you feel sick after sex (women), or if you become queasy at the site of blood and gore, that's your vagus nerve over-stimulating.

One of the most common ways people stimulate their vagus nerve is by simply going to the bathroom. When we strain a bit to push, we tighten our stomach muscles and stimulate the nerve. This is why we feel more relaxed afterward. The immediate feeling of relief is because we stimulated the relief nerve.

Current research has shown that stimulating the vagus nerve can produce positive effects in conditions like: epilepsy with seizures, migraines, obesity, insomnia, diabetes, poor blood circulation, heart disease, high blood pressure, fibromyalgia, OCD, inflammation, multiple sclerosis, Alzheimer's disease, depression, anxiety, and other mental and mood disorders.

It's very promising to know that the body has an internal balancing system that is so easily triggered through deliberate actions. It's even more promising to know that countless studies have shown its positive effects on common and widespread disorders.

Offer the body stress without resolution or relief and it will begin to throw one of your systems off balance, which will throw another system off balance and another. If you interrupt the process of restoration and rejuvenation, then your body can't do what its designed to do.

Offer the body relief and it will begin the process of balancing and restoring normal functioning in all areas. Offer the body relief consistently for a longer period of time and 70-90% of all stress related illness will cure themselves. It all begins with a little bit of relief.

This book will offer you ease and relief through passages, statements, and exercises. The relief passages are designed to make you feel better about your life, your progress, your choices, or about yourself as a whole. They are created to bring you ease and help you let go more. This will help you emotionally and mentally to make better choices and create the results you prefer.

Some of the exercises will help you discharge built-up resistance, some will help you continue to stay relaxed, and others will help you to prevent future activation. Most will help you by stimulating your vagus nerve. The more you practice them, the more resilience you will build toward stress.

This book offers you words for your mind and exercises for your body. Together, this book combines mind and body relief to bring you results you can feel as you read and practice it. If you would like lasting results, please practice the exercises until they become a habit. Peace is cultivated through practice.

Relief will help your body, your mind, your emotions, your health, your ability to make better choices, your relationships, and your overall life. Once this practice becomes a habit, you will see and feel the difference in all of those areas.

Relief is a habit. Relaxation is a habit. Calm is a habit. Peace is a habit. We can create those habits in one of two ways: 1. By releasing what causes us stress. Or 2. By actively working on our peace and relaxation. This book offers you both options. The work is up to you.

PART 2
PASSAGES AND STATEMENTS

Relief Passages

Note:

As you read the following passages, pay close attention to where you feel relief in your body. Does your chest feel lighter? Do your muscles feel less tense? Does your breathing change? Do you experience heat or tingling? Stay mindful of your bodily changes.

You're not behind in life. There's no schedule or timetable that we all must follow. It's all made up. Wherever you are right now is exactly where you need to be. Seven billion people can't do everything in exactly the same scheduled order. We are all different with a variety of needs and goals. Some get married early, some get married late, while others don't get married at all. What is early? What is late? Compared with whom? Compared with what? Some want children, others don't. Some want a career; others enjoy taking care of a house and children. Your life is not on anyone else's schedule. Don't beat yourself up for where you are right now. It's YOUR timeline, not anyone else's, and nothing is off schedule.

You're not a bad person for having negative thoughts or feelings. You're not getting it wrong or failing in life. You're not less spiritual, less human, or less evolved for going through an emotional funk or for feeling stuck. At your core, you are a learning and growing being. And you are doing just that.

The Book of Relief

It's okay if you made a choice you are no longer happy about. It's not necessarily a mistake. You've simply grown from that moment and now you have different ideas, needs, and beliefs, and you want something more suited for who you are currently. This is a normal process of life. Don't punish yourself for growing. You're allowed to change your mind. Your desires and needs are allowed to evolve into something different.

Where there are inflictors of pain, there are also healers of the damage. Where there are promoters of violence, there are also walkers of peace. Where there are breeders of hate, there are also sowers of love. Humanity only appears hopeless when we focus on the negatives. Focus on those who help each other and heal each other. Focus on those who shine a light in the darkness. Hope or despair can be found in every situation; it just depends on which one we look for.

The Book of Relief

You did the best you could with the knowledge you had in that moment. It's easier to look back at an event and see a better choice or pathway because we already learned from our experience. Hindsight happens after the lesson, so we can't condemn ourselves for not knowing the lesson before we learned it.

Progression is part regression. Moving forward sometimes involves taking a few steps back during the process. Nothing has gone wrong. This is how we all move forward. Every project has setbacks. Every plan runs into a wall every once in a while. Every relationship has miscommunications and conflicts. Some days you will wake up feeling good; other days you will feel off. You will lose some money; you will gain some money. You will lose some weight; you will gain some weight. All of life is a process of expansion and contraction. This is how life breathes.

Most of life is an ongoing process of learning. We don't stop learning once we grow out of childhood and we don't stop learning once we finish school. Learning is not necessarily a painful process but it can be when we internally punish or abuse ourselves for mistakes. We do this when we forget that:

1. We are always learning.

2. Mistakes are a part of the process of learning.

3. If we knew the right answer, we would use the right answer.

4. Sometimes, the right answer is only revealed by choosing the wrong answer.

5. Maybe then, it wasn't the wrong answer after all.

We resist what we don't want. However, sometimes knowing what you don't want puts you in a better position to understand the fullness of what you do want. It's a clarifying process that helps you in the long run because it offers you the opportunity right now to adjust your actions and results. So if you can think of every experience as either fulfilling a desire or clarifying a desire, then you will never resist another moment ever again because each one benefits you by helping you shape your overall future.

It's okay if you don't have all the right answers. No one does. There is not a single person alive or dead who knew every right decision to make and when to make it. Most people just do the best they can with what they know in the moment. Most people just follow their gut and hope it works out well. Sometimes, it does; sometimes, it doesn't. The difference between happiness and suffering is how you treat yourself when it doesn't. You're going to make many choices that don't work out, so you might as well be kind to yourself when they don't. It'll help you bounce back faster and move forward sooner.

When we narrow in on one moment on this long never-ending journey, we mistakenly conclude that something did or didn't work out for us. We become too specific and rigid in the outcome we desire and don't realize that it's an ongoing process that never ends. One outcome is the opening of the path to another. If we can become more flexible in how we get there and what "there" looks like, if we can pull back our perspective a bit and realize it's always in the process of happening, then we might find that everything has been working out for us all along.

Self-love is most needed when we are least likely to give it. When we feel defeated, hopeless, wrong, or like a failure; that's when it's most important. That's when it makes a difference. It's easy to love yourself when you say the right things, or get the best laugh for a joke, when you finish a project, or look good in that dress. You most need it when you say the wrong thing, when you don't get that laugh, when your project fails, when you don't look good in that dress. That's when it truly counts.

Unconditional self-love means loving ourselves in the moments we think we shouldn't. It means giving ourselves the benefit of the doubt. It means forgiving ourselves and being kind regardless of the results. Self-love is really self-compassion. It's okay if you didn't get it right, you will have many more chances and opportunities to do so. If you hurt or abuse yourself emotionally or mentally, you'll never grow. You'll only add more wounds. You don't deserve that. Give yourself some love, attention, and kindness and watch how fast you will turn it around.

The Book of Relief

Some things fall apart so that other things can fall together. This is the nature of life. We can view it from our short-term perspective or we can trust the long-term process of creation. Nothing new can come about without including pieces of something that once was. A nebula explodes scattering its debris across the universe. It appears as if something has gone wrong, but this is how new worlds are created.

The Book of Relief

Just because you're in the process of bettering yourself doesn't mean there won't be times when you make questionable choices, respond out of character, lack proper communication, or let negativity get the best of yourself. That's all a part of the process of becoming better. How else would you know what needs cleaning up if you don't stand in your mess every once in a while?

We all have issues we need to work on and wounds that still require healing. But just because you still have lessons to learn in some areas doesn't mean you don't have lessons to teach in other areas. We all have the ability and experience to be teachers for what we've mastered. However, we're also students for things we have yet to understand. You've been through a lot and you can teach a lot to others, even if you're in the process of learning yourself. Give yourself a break if you're having a hard time in some areas. You can be really good at some things and not-so-good at others. It's all a part of being a whole human.

If some things didn't work out the way you wanted them to, then perhaps they worked out the way they needed to. We might know what's best for us but we don't always see the path that will get us there. Maybe the path has a car accident or a loss of a job. Maybe the path is through a divorce. Maybe the path is through moving to a completely different city. Even though the path might have some pain or struggle on it, it doesn't mean that it's not leading to your best life.

Don't beat yourself up for having a negative thought or feeling. That only feeds the negativity and ensures its place in your mind. Expect that you will feel some intense or uncomfortable feelings and let them pass when they come up. Don't judge them and don't judge yourself for experiencing them. When you resist them, they take root inside you; when you welcome them, they pass through you. Let them come, let them go.

The Book of Relief

Ride the wave of confusion. Ride the wave of frustration. Ride the wave of anger. Just go with it. Regardless of how you feel, accept it. It transforms faster that way. Find a way to be okay with everything not being okay, and everything will be okay.

Pessimists are always right. That's why they can't change their lives or the world. They stop the moment something falls flat or fails. They stop the moment it all goes wrong because that's when they're right. There's no reason or motivation for them to keep moving forward or to try another way. There's no stake in success or perseverance because they're only right in the wrong. Don't listen to people who tell you all the ways it can go wrong. They may be right about some setbacks but there's always another chance and another way past it. The obstacle is not the finish line. All you have to do is keep moving forward from the setback, and you can find a way through.

Don't complicate the process of change by overthinking it and then talking yourself out of it. Just begin somewhere. Begin where you feel the most comfortable no matter how small of a step it is. As long as you start the process and keep it going with small steps, you'll build momentum and confidence as you go. It's better to take a small step every day for a month than one large step once a month. Small steps will teach you consistency, which is the foundation of real change. When large steps encounter setbacks, they carry bigger consequences and pushback, but small steps are easier to adjust. It doesn't matter if you don't radically change your life in one month because real change doesn't happen that fast. It happens day in and day out with small steps that eventually build up to big changes. Take it one day at a time.

What helped you survive back then can hold you back now. What was meant to be a temporary coping mechanism might have become a pattern of behavior that contributes to your current suffering. You no longer need to protect yourself through disconnection, distrust, and numbness. You are not that person anymore, and those habits are no longer needed for protection. You can take care of yourself now. You are older, wiser, and more experienced than before. Trust yourself; you can handle much more than you give yourself credit for. Trust your experiences and what they taught you. Trust your growth and your newfound strength. You can do this. You are better now. Trust it.

Your emotions are valid. You have a right to be angry about what you experienced. You have a right to be sad about what happened. When you accept and own your emotions, you will naturally move through them. If you deny or wrong them, then you'll continue to be stuck in them. Judging your emotions prolongs them and creates cycles of shame and anger. You have a right to feel how you feel, regardless of why you feel it. Let it happen. Accept it. Allow it to do what it needs to do. And when you're ready, let it go.

If someone is criticizing you, ask yourself: do they truly love you? Do they support you? Do they respect you? Do they trust you to make the right decisions? Do they know you well enough to know what's best for you? If the answer is no to any of these questions, then it doesn't matter what they have to say to you or about you. It won't be coming from a place of love or support. It won't be well-rounded advice or constructive criticism because they don't know the intricacies of you.

Most of the time, people vent their own frustrations through your life choices. They criticize your progress because they're not making any of their own. It's not meant to make you feel better; it's meant to make themselves feel better. If they don't have your best interests in mind, then pay no mind. It simply doesn't matter what they have to say.

The Book of Relief

Anything in nature that blooms eventually withers and falls apart. After some time and nourishment, it blooms once again. It goes through this cycle over and over again. So do we. We have our own seasons full of working/planting, nurturing/growing, enjoying/reaping, retracting/withering, and then rest and replenishment so we can start again. There's nothing wrong with any of those stages. They all serve their purpose in the long run.

When you're having a moment of negativity, just let yourself have it. Stop punishing yourself for your human side. It's only natural. Of course we're going to get angry when we experience unfairness or injustice. Of course we're going to be saddened by tragedy or loss. Give yourself time and space to feel what you feel. Then, when you're done, pick yourself back up and carry on.

The irony is that unconditional self-love fuels self-transformation. When you get to the point of pure acceptance of all that you are, including the darkness, the flaws, and the mistakes, you no longer feel the need to change yourself into something better. And that's when all the changes take place.

The more you fight for a "better" you—the type of better that comes from self-judgment—the more you prolong the changes that come from radical self-acceptance. When you love and accept yourself even though you're not better, you automatically become better. Your mood improves. You feel more energetic. You make different choices. You feel confident and more at ease. Your behavior changes because the energy you spent hating the aspects of yourself you couldn't accept is now free to be utilized in other ways. You will feel lighter, freer, and more at peace than you have ever felt before. When you accept yourself, you open the doors to your own prison.

Give yourself time to heal. Whether it's from something physical, emotional, mental, or spiritual, healing has its own timeline and can't be rushed. If you become impatient and frustrated, you're going to add more stress into your body and mind, which will slow down the healing process. You will create the opposite of your desire. Give yourself permission to take your time. Give yourself permission to get it right. The only fast track to healing is through self-compassion, self-love, self-forgiveness, and self-care, and none of those things can be rushed or done sloppily.

Not all experiences are meant to last. In fact, most experiences are nothing more than another step in the clarifying process. Without experience, we can't know what we truly desire. Was there ever a time when you were so sure you wanted something, only to change your mind after you received it? The experience wasn't a mistake; you didn't choose wrong. It was a clarifying process. Now you know which aspects of the experience you want and which ones you don't. Growth happens as we sort through a variety of experiences and become clear in who we are and what we want.

Life isn't as bad as it seems in the moment of frustration. Stress can restrict our focus to a small window of possibilities and narrow our vision of potential resolutions. Frustration is a sign that we can't see another way through our current struggle. However, this doesn't mean there isn't another way through. Just because we can't see the possibility right now doesn't mean it doesn't exist. There are many avenues and paths that can open from where we stand. Reality is not as limited as our minds perceive it to be. Sometimes, you have to let the solution find you.

There is no loss in life, only a trade. We give up one thing with the intention of gaining another, even when we're not aware of our intention. It has always been this way. We trade the comfort of our parents' home for the journey of growth and independence by moving out. We trade a constricting relationship for the feeling of freedom and individuality by choosing to become single again. We trade the safety of a job we don't like for a stronger sense of integrity and purpose through entrepreneurship.

When we are willing to let go of one thing for another, there is no real loss. We are really choosing another option that feels better for us in that particular period of our lives. In this sense, we never lose the things we gave up—we simply trade them to gain something better.

It doesn't matter that you reacted the way you did when you did. What matters is that you now understand that there was another option. What matters is that you're now open to changing your reactions. What matters is that you have learned from that experience and you're open to doing better. Punishing yourself won't change your future reactions for the better. It'll only make you feel bad about yourself, which will ensure that you continue to have negative reactions. Give yourself a break.

Even those who become an overnight success have been doing the work for years without much attention or glory. Just because we don't see how much they have struggled doesn't mean they didn't. Keep doing the work; your time will come when the struggle starts to become easier. Success comes to those who make the work a part of themselves instead of seeing it as something outside of themselves that needs to be forced or manipulated into compliance. It's not something you do; it's who you are. Keep doing the work until it no longer feels like work.

The experience doesn't change you. You change yourself based on how you interpret the experience. If you see it as evidence of your bad luck, you'll begin to expect more negative experiences and that will alter the way you behave with each following experience. However, if you see it as an opportunity, then you'll be more open with each new experience. Either way, it's not the experience that determines who you are; it's who you are that determines the experience.

Most major decisions are made several times over a long period of time. There are no final choices that are made in one moment and carry over forever after. Even when you decide once and for all that you're going to eat healthy or quit smoking, it's still a decision you will have to make every day. It's still a choice in the moment when you pick the broccoli over the chips or when you choose to chew gum instead of smoking a cigarette. When you choose your spouse in one moment during your vows, you still wake up every day making the choice to stay together instead of giving up.

We might make the initial choice with determination, but there will be days when it will feel harder. We might struggle more to stay on track. If you slip up at one point and choose something that goes against your initial choice, don't make that mean you failed. Everyone does it at some point. Sometimes, you choose the chips. Sometimes, you sneak a cigarette. Sometimes, you give up in your relationship. The only point that matters is: what will you do now? Will you continue to stay on track, or will you quit? Only you can decide that.

The Book of Relief

Everything is going to be okay. We don't always believe that in the midst of pain and suffering, but no state is ever permanent. Once the high of the initial shock or drama calms down, things will return to normal again. They always do. The sun will rise tomorrow, the birds will sing, the trees will sway, and you will eat your breakfast and go about your life.

If you can trust that it's always working out for you, even when it feels like it's not, then you can trust that each moment is leading you to where you need to be, even if it's not necessarily where you want to be. And if you find yourself in a moment you absolutely don't want to be in, remember that one road leads to another and another. A few detours or roadblocks are not the end of the line. There's always another way. There's always a clearing just up ahead if you keep moving.

Experience adds value and clarity, regardless of the outcome. Everything that happens isn't just about getting something tangible like a relationship, money, job, or possessions. Sometimes, it's about learning something we need to know before we can get to where we're going. Sometimes, we need all the experiences that came before so we can become the person we need to be to handle what we truly want. Trust that you're on your path and that nothing has gone wrong.

The Book of Relief

Every decision leads to another and another and another. There is no moment when we are not choosing something over another. If you make a decision that you don't like or agree with, you have multiple opportunities to make multiple choices. There is always another choice that follows that one.

The Book of Relief

Everyone doesn't learn, grow, or understand at the same pace. In some regards, we learn faster, and in others, we learn slower. Neither means anything. Being faster isn't necessarily better. Being slower isn't necessarily worse. Everything happens in its own time. Let it take its course.

Often times, we don't see how brave or strong we are when we are in the midst of struggle. We only see what we can't do, what our shortcomings are, and how we said the wrong things. The mere fact that you've encountered struggles in the past is proof that you are smarter and stronger than before. Every experience teaches us something, even when we aren't aware of the lesson. Trust that you are stronger. You are smarter. This problem might seem big, but it's not bigger than you.

A problem is a narrowing of perspective. Nothing is ever as big, bad, or terrible as we think it is when we are going through it. Our emotions usually cloud our ability to see things clearly, which makes it appear to be worse than it is. The magnitude of a problem is determined by our ability or inability to see a solution. When we have the answer to a problem, it doesn't feel like much of a problem. Even the biggest dilemma in our lives doesn't seem as bad when we can see a way out of it. How it feels is generally determined by how we perceive it. It's not the size or range of the problem that determines how bad it is; it's the span of our perception of the whole picture.

Up has down, darkness has light, in has out, east has west, yin has yang, and a problem has a solution. Everything exists in a balance of opposites because life is whole. Neither one is good nor bad; it's simply one part of a big mosaic. We deem things good or bad based on which part we currently see, how we see it, and which aspects we pay close attention to. There is a solution to everything, but first you have to believe there is. What you don't believe can't come to you. Trust that there is a balance and wholeness within everything, including yourself.

Sometimes, we grow out of relationships, jobs, situations, and beliefs. When we were younger, we grew out of our school grades and advanced because we knew more and that required different challenges so we could continue to grow. The same is true for life. You might grow out of your old self and your old life. You could punish yourself for it or you could embrace it. The same way you embraced your transition from the 4th grade to the 5th. It was a natural progression of your growth and life as a child, and it was celebrated. So celebrate it now. We never stop growing up.

Think of a difficulty or challenge as a seed planted in the dirt. It may seem dark momentarily, and it may seem as if nothing is moving forward; however, over time, that seed bears fruit. Our challenges change us even if we can't see the process just yet. It happens little by little each day. Every difficulty adds more nourishment and beauty in our overall garden of life. One day, very soon from now, you'll look out and see how each one complements and supports the other. You'll marvel at how it all came together and just how perfect and beautiful it all is.

Sometimes, you have to decide that your mental health and overall wellbeing is more important than whatever you're stressing about. Sometimes, you have to make a conscious decision to choose yourself. Sometimes, you just have to let it go and let it be whatever it is. Give yourself that freedom.

The Book of Relief

So you tried something, you reached for something, you pursued something, and it didn't work. It doesn't matter. The point is that you were brave enough to go after what you wanted in the first place. Bravery is one of the best characteristics for success, even if you didn't get it yet. Stay brave, and it will lead you to your desired outcome; if not this time around, then soon enough. Fortune favors the brave.

When we don't feel good in the present, we hate our past and the events that have brought us to this current moment. When we feel joy in the present, we feel gratitude for our past and all the events that have brought us to this moment. The past doesn't change either way. How we see and feel about our past depends on how we feel now. Regardless of what happened then, we can always feel better now because the past doesn't exist in the present. We either use it as justification or motivation, and that choice is always up to us in this moment.

In life, you'll have moments of uncertainty when you're just don't know what to do or what to choose. You'll be confused and unsure. Those moments are rare opportunities of possibility. Most of the time, we know what we will decide before it's even presented to us. We're so sure of what we want or don't want that we rarely sit in the openness of possibility. But in the moments when we're uncertain, in the moments of confusion, anything is possible. Instead of letting that paralyze you, let it inspire you and open you up to a new pathway. It just might be exactly what you need right now.

Nothing is worth the damage of self-abuse. It solves no problem, accomplishes no goal, and helps no one. It has no benefit or productive value. It serves only one purpose: to make you feel bad, which doesn't help you or anyone else. We are more likely to emotionally resign, mentally disengage, or stop trying when we feel bad about ourselves. It does not motivate or inspire us to do better; instead, it disempowers us from moving forward because we stop trusting ourselves to make the right choices. If it can be changed, fixed, or forgiven, then mentally abusing yourself is unnecessary. If it can't be changed, fixed, or forgiven, then mentally abusing yourself is pointless. Offer yourself some compassion as you move through life. Of course you're not going to have all the right answers. That's how we learn. Don't beat yourself up for a very human and very normal process.

It's okay if you're tired. It's okay if you said something you now wish you hadn't. It's okay if you made a mistake, had a breakdown, or couldn't do what you wanted to. It's okay; it's okay. Dwelling on any of those experiences will only prolong them and make you feel worse. The only thing that matters is: what are you going to do today? What now? Focus there and leave all the other stuff behind.

We do what we can do when we can do it. Don't expect so much from yourself that you fall short every time. That won't help you move forward. It will discourage you from trying other things. Instead, break down bigger tasks into many smaller tasks and take those on one by one. There is no rush because there is no finish line. Take your time and be easy with yourself.

You are a living, breathing, organic being. Of course you can feel pain, of course you can feel hurt, of course it feels overwhelming sometimes as the jagged, rough, and hard world outside bumps up against your soft skin. You are not a machine that rams through each experience, performing tasks with no emotions. You are alive. You are alive. You are alive. Be kind to this soft creature as it learns its way around a busy and loud world. Be easy with yourself because some days you'll be the only one who is. But that's okay because you're the only one that makes a real difference.

We become so complacent with our lives that change sometimes feels wrong. We grow so used to how easily certain things operate that we begin to feel discord from growth. When something veers off in a direction we weren't expecting or desiring, we conclude that something must have gone wrong. We immediately judge it and wrestle with it, trying to manipulate it into our idea of how it should be. We try to recreate the old, thinking it will spare us from the uncomfortable and painful feeling of growth. We want things to stay the same because change feels uncertain and uneasy. But perhaps, nothing has gone wrong at all. Perhaps, everything is in a state of growth and it was just time for more progress. It's only just beginning to move in a better direction, but if we judge it prematurely and then try to stop it from coming about, we just might end up fighting our own blessings.

The Book of Relief

Every problem doesn't have a solution; it has multiple solutions, ways, paths, and avenues to better circumstances and resolutions. You don't have to worry about finding the one and only solution that exists for that problem. There are multiple possibilities, and the first step to finding one is to stop worrying about it. First, find some ease in your body and allow your mind to relax. Then, the next right step will become so obvious, you'll wonder why you didn't think of it before.

Peace is okay. Calm is okay. It's okay to feel relief. It's okay to allow yourself to relax. You don't have to be on edge all the time. You don't have to be ready for the next stressful event. It's okay if you let go a bit and allow yourself some rest. It's okay if you take some time for yourself. Nothing will fall apart or go wrong. In fact, things will work much better after you're relaxed and rested.

Life feels easier when we learn to let go of controlling our unfolding circumstances. The feelings of struggle and heaviness come from resisting our current experiences. We resist because we don't understand why change needs to occur. We resist because the unfamiliar can feel painful and uncomfortable. We resist because we don't trust ourselves to navigate through the maze of new information and experiences. But if we can learn to let go a little, if we can learn to trust our innate ability to adapt and survive, if we can find a bit of ease and relaxation, then we can enter into the new phases of our lives without bringing the old painful habits of resistance with us.

We get so used to looking for what's wrong around us that we forget to appreciate what's right, what's good, and what comes easy. What works well is hardly ever noticed because it's working well. It doesn't require our attention or focus, unlike something that suddenly stops working. It's only then that we begin to take notice. Two or three things not working can feel like our whole lives are off balance. However, there is much more working in our lives than not. There is much more health in our bodies than illness. If these statements weren't true, we wouldn't be alive. Once that balance truly tips over to the negative side, life can't be sustained. If you are alive, there is much more balance, wellness, and goodness in your life than you realize.

Forgive yourself for how you chose to survive. Forgive yourself for the desires you judged harshly. Forgive yourself for indulging in things that took up your time but didn't fulfill you. Forgive yourself for declaring yourself as someone you're not. Forgive yourself for your chosen avenues of negative expression. Forgive yourself for all the times you didn't add value to others. Forgive yourself for what you discovered about yourself that you didn't like. Forgive yourself for whatever ugliness you saw in yourself. Forgive yourself for not correcting what you think you should have. Forgive yourself for the parts you couldn't respect. Forgive yourself for all these judgments. Forgive yourself for not being able to forgive yourself before.

The Book of Relief

It's usually not as bad as we initially think it is. Our minds are designed to first think up the worst-case scenario because that's how survival works. We think we're preparing ourselves when, in reality, we're just complicating the issues further. Most things work themselves out without our interference. Most things don't require a reaction. Most things aren't as bad as we think they are.

The Book of Relief

No power on this earth can change or decide how you feel about yourself. You're the one who decides you're not good enough, you're the one who decides you should be punished or shamed. You're the one who decides to listen to, accept, and believe other people's opinions of you. You can let that go at any moment and immediately feel better about yourself.

It's time to let go of the idea that you somehow deserve pain or punishment for your past choices. You don't have to keep reliving them and hurting yourself with it. Torturing yourself doesn't help you or anyone else. It doesn't change anything that happened before, and it doesn't teach you anything in the now. True growth is making better choices in the present because you learned from your past behavior. Redemption is not measured by how much you suffer; it's measured by how much you've grown from who you used to be.

Sometimes, the best option is to do nothing. Sometimes, the only reaction is one of no reaction. Sometimes, it's simply vital to leave things be and let it go. We don't always have to accept the invitation to engage with every conflict. We don't need to feed the drama or enter the argument. When we disengage from negativity and choose our own wellbeing over continuing to feed cycles of reoccurring conflicts, we take an important much-needed step in our healing.

Negative thinking is like walking around in a warm coat during the summer because you're expecting winter to come sometime in the future. You're not wrong for wanting to be prepared for it, but is it helpful to wear a winter coat during the summer? That's what you do when you fill your mind with negative thoughts as things are going well for you. You think you're preparing yourself for what might happen when all you do is make things unnecessarily difficult for yourself in the present. You make yourself uncomfortable, frustrated, and upset for no real reason. It's possible to enjoy the winter, to thrive in winter, to have fun in winter. So take the coat off and have trust that you know what to do when it happens. Allow yourself to enjoy the summer, then winter won't feel so bad when it arrives.

The Book of Relief

It's okay if you don't feel okay. If you feel angry, feel angry. If you feel sad, feel sad. Don't make yourself wrong for what comes up from within you. If it's there, it's there. It won't just disappear because you don't want it anymore. It goes away when it's allowed, when it's felt, when it's given permission to pass through. Welcome what you feel, and soon enough it will disappear.

You're allowed to grow. You're allowed to change. You're allowed to have new desires. You're allowed to have varying needs. You're allowed to change your mind and beliefs. You're allowed to think new thoughts. You're allowed to be different from what people are used to experiencing from you. You're allowed to be anything you already are or are in the process of becoming. This is your right as an evolving human being.

Problems appear to be bad because they feel like threats to our wellbeing, our relationships, or our financial security. They feel like unnecessary invaders that have come to mess up our lives. However, problems better our lives by forcing us into growth. If we want to overcome the problem, then we have to become better than who we were when the problem first appeared. We have to think differently, use other resources, or find other paths. We become sharper, smarter, and more resourceful. We learn something new through each encounter with a problem. We are pushed into becoming better. We pick up more and more helpful characteristics that aid us in avoiding future problems that are similar in nature. We also become more patient, more kind, and more wise. But most importantly, we become more useful to others because of our newfound knowledge and experience.

You don't have to know exactly where you're going or how you're going to get there. Sometimes, when we get into the specifics, we end up talking ourselves out of the journey before we even start. It begins to feel too hard or like too much work to get every element to line up in our favor. We are often looking too far ahead and planning for things that probably won't even happen. However, if we just begin walking in the general direction of where we want to be and allow the path to offer us more specific signs along the way, then we can reach our destination one signpost at a time. The only required elements are the belief and trust that the destination exists, that it's possible to get there somehow, and that we can handle whatever obstacles show up on our path. As you begin the journey in the general direction of where you want to be, you will encounter people and situations that will help you become clearer in your next step. We can call them signposts, obstacles, or guides, or we can call them opportunities for clarity. Either way, everything along the way will help you understand what you want more clearly and which connecting road will take you further.

If you end up doing only one thing from this entire book, let it be this: stop being angry with yourself. That alone is enough to radically alter your health, your relationships, your job, and your life. Don't be angry with yourself for not saying the right thing. Don't be angry with yourself for forgetting to do something you said you would do. Don't be angry with yourself for not finishing that project as fast as everyone else at work. Don't be angry with yourself for finishing school late, for being unemployed, for being single. Don't be angry with yourself for not saying what you wanted to say or not doing what you wanted to do. Regardless of what choices you have made, let go of the habit of self-anger. It doesn't serve you. It never has and it never will.

Every time you get angry with yourself for where you are in your process of growth, it's the equivalent of chopping off the head of the rose because it hasn't bloomed yet. Now you have to go through that part of the process again. Anger will set you back every time and slow down your growth. However, self-compassion and self-encouragement are like water and sunshine; they help the growth process happen faster and easier. It's up to you how you want to proceed, but if you can break the habit of getting angry with yourself and replace it with some compassion and encouragement, then you will bloom like you have never bloomed before.

If we were all doctors, then we would have no hospitals to work in without architects or construction workers. We would have no cars to get to our patients without engineers and mechanics. We would have no tools or electronics to work with, no medicine to heal with, no textbooks to study from, no teachers to teach us, no school to learn in, and then we couldn't be doctors. Every one is blessed with a special skill, talent, or gift and when we put them all together, it makes the grand human puzzle complete. We are all important for the gifts we give to this world. Whether you are a doctor, taxi driver, janitor, waiter, or painter, you are a blessing to this world. You are important to the whole of humanity. Honor yourself.

Sometimes, life pulls you into your ultimate becoming through a divorce, job loss, health crisis, or some other misunderstood means. We might not like the process; however, it just might be the fastest or best route to our highest self. Growth can be painful, but the outcome is always aligned with our highest good. We get to choose whether we resist the process and make it harder on ourselves or whether we trust that we are ultimately getting what is right for us, even if we can't see it right now. We can't control how we get there, but we can control whether we're angry and bitter or relaxed and trusting on the way.

The Book of Relief

It's not a question of whether you grow or don't. That's inevitable. As you live your life, you're going to have experiences and grow from them. That's your natural state. It's a question of whether it's going to be a hard or easy process. It's a question of whether it's going to be painful or enjoyable. The answer to that depends on how willing you are, how open you are, and how much ease you experience.

The body is always in the present moment, beating your heart, pumping your blood, making new cells. Its only focus is to keep you alive right now. That is the only reality it experiences. It has no concern for what has happened before or what could happen later. It exists in a current state of harmony. However, we disturb its peace by remembering and stressing out about events that are not currently transpiring in front of us. When we carry the past into the present moment or when we imagine a negative future event, we disturb the body's present-moment functioning and introduce discord through our thoughts. Your body knows how to return to balance, wellness, and rejuvenation. All you have to do is take your mind off of the past and the future. Bring it here and now where you are safe. Bring it here and now where there is balance, and peace, and calm.

If you want to be seen, you have to be yourself. Otherwise, what is being seen? The characteristics of other people you've determined are better than your own? The fragments of whatever illusions others pass on as reality? What is it that you want others to see? Is it the you that is you? Or is it the composite you that is made from the pieces of all the people you've deemed as worthy of owning their authenticity? You can't absorb their true self; you can only claim your own. You not only have a right to be who you are, but you have a right to be seen and celebrated, even with all the cracks and bruises. They don't make you any less real, wonderful, or deserving. They come together to create the fullness that is you, and you won't be able to find that you in anyone else ever. That's a beautiful thing.

You don't only outgrow people, places, and jobs. You also outgrow yourself. You outgrow your old beliefs, old thought patterns, and old identities, as well. One day, you find that you're not the person you once thought you were. And the new person you've become simply doesn't want to work at that boring job, or continue to be friends with that toxic person, or stay in that constraining place anymore. They're not a match for who you've become, and it simply won't last any longer.

Transition periods are only hard when we can't let go of our previous life states, even though our previous mental and emotional states have evolved. Then, we feel stuck because we're trying to move forward and stay behind at the same time. Guilt and obligation can hold us back, even though we are ready for the next stage in our lives. When you can feel that it's time to move on, then it's time to move on. If you let go and have faith in the process, life will bring you so much more than you have ever had before.

The shortest day of the year, also known as the darkest day of the year, is the culmination of Earth's annual darkness cycle. This is when winter begins. However, it also triggers the beginning of the cycle of light, where each day adds a little bit more daytime as we move forward toward the longest day of the year, which has the most light. Then the cycle begins again for darkness.

Everything in nature goes through cycles of blooming and withering, light and dark, growth and decay. Everything flows with nature's rule of contrast and balance. We all go through these periods, as well. What helps ease the process is having someone to guide, support, or help us through it. Which is why it's important that when we end up on the reaping part of the cycle, we help someone who's on the sowing side. As you feel better, it will put you in a better position to help others, as well.

There is no right or wrong way to live your life. It's simply a matter of what works for you and what doesn't work for you. And if it works for you, then it's right for you. Whether you marry early, marry late, have six children or none; whether you work your whole life or never work at all. None of these choices are right or wrong in and of themselves. They only feel wrong when we compare our choices to other people's choices. They only feel wrong when other people try to advise us into what works for them. However, what works for others might not work for you and vice versa.

You won't know if something is right for you strictly based on what felt right for other people. You have to listen to your own instincts. Exploration will lead you to new conclusions and preferences. Then, you can decide what is right for you. And even if, in the end, you come to the realization that it was not for you, it was still beneficial because it added to your experience and knowledge of self. Whether it worked for you or didn't work for you, you are never wrong for exploring and growing. That's how you discover who you are.

Do what you can and let go of what you can't. If you are able to extend a hand to someone, if you are able to give your time or energy, if you are able to offer advice, then do so. If, however, you can't do either or any of those things, then don't beat yourself up for it. You can't help everyone, you can't save everyone, and you can't be there for everyone. It's impossible for one person to do everything. Trust that what you do is enough and don't carry the weight of those you couldn't help as a burden upon your shoulders.

Your lacks are not justification for self-abuse; all that does is put you in a position of not being able to help anyone else because you've disabled yourself. When you are gentle with yourself, you will be more gentle with others. When you develop deep compassion for yourself, you will amass deep compassion for others. When you learn to love yourself, you will be able to teach others the same. The first step in being able to help as many people as possible is to first help yourself.

Tomorrow's flower is today's seed. And it's okay that the seed is not a flower yet. It's okay that it has a bit of a process to undertake before it blooms. There's nothing wrong with the seed right now. It's exactly what it's supposed to be in this moment. And so are you.

The Book of Relief

Whether you feel your absolute best or your absolute worst today, you still deserve comfort, care, and love. You still deserve the kindness of strangers and the compassion of good friends. You still deserve hearty belly laughs and a good night's sleep. You still deserve warm baths and a night out to your favorite restaurant. You still deserve those little moments that make you feel glad you were there to witness them. Regardless of how you feel, you will always remain a deserving being worthy of the best moment that is possible for you right here and right now.

The Book of Relief

Children don't learn how to walk the first time they try, and yet they don't give up just because they continuously fall down. They keep doing it until they get it. And once they get it, their entire world is different because now they've advanced from crawling to walking. Even though they experienced pain and a bit of frustration, their lives are now better because they can get to their destination faster and easier. They know that the benefit of walking outweighs the temporary pain of falling down.

Our instincts show up as a feeling in our gut. So when we are overly stressed, we overwork our gut and can't feel the right answer because it's bombarded with too many emotions and stressful thoughts. Sometimes, a little time and space away from a problem can bring so much more clarity. Once your mind and body find ease and relief, then they can help you find the right answer and the next appropriate step forward.

The world can be an unforgiving place; this is why you must learn to forgive yourself. This is why you must learn to give yourself permission to want what you want and to go after it with everything you have. This is why you must learn to give yourself the love you crave, the kindness you yearn for, and the compassion you need. This is why you must fill the lacks you discover with something other than criticism, hate, or anger. This is why you must forgive yourself—because that's how you become whole again.

The Book of Relief

You understand more now than you ever did before. You are the culmination of all that you have experienced in the past. You are at your highest state of wisdom and strength in this moment. Everything that happened helped you to become who you are now. And even though that person might feel incomplete or broken at times, you are more complete now than you have ever been before. Let your completion continue to unfold as it is. It's going to be a miraculous and beautiful unfolding.

Sometimes, you take a few steps back. It doesn't mean you have failed. It doesn't mean that you're headed in the wrong direction. Nothing has gone wrong. It's a natural part of the journey. Sometimes, you stop. Sometimes, you rest. Sometimes, you take a few steps back to retrieve something you need. Let go of your expectations and don't judge yourself for delays, detours, or unexpected guests. It's all a part of the process.

Maybe it was hard before. Maybe you didn't know what to do or who to turn to. Maybe you wished and prayed for better days. Maybe it seemed like it would never end. But you survived. You survived. You did what you needed to do, and you made it. You are so much more courageous and stronger and smarter than you give yourself credit for. You are so much kinder and more compassionate than you realize. The fact that you even want to beat yourself up for how you handled your past shows that you believe you could have been a better person. Only good people feel that way. Only good people believe they could have been better. Only good people want to be better. So be good to yourself. Let it go and let yourself be better. It doesn't start with you hurting yourself; it starts with you being good to yourself. You deserve it.

No one is completely sure of the outcome before they make a decision. No one knows with 100% certainty what kind of results their actions will bring. We follow our instincts, we navigate through our internal compass, we use our previous experiences as tools, and we hope for the best. As we move forward, we adjust our actions based on the type of results we get. That's all any of us can do. So if you're unsure, you're one of us. If you don't know, we don't either. If you're trying the best you can and hoping for the best to occur, so are we.

Confusion is a crucial part of the growth process. It pushes us to inquire more, to discover more, to look deeper into things. It engages our curiosity and stimulates our willingness to be open. As we become more confused, our desire for clarity grows stronger, helping us to push past whatever barriers we have set up so we can venture into new territory. It turns us into seekers. In that respect, confusion serves an important purpose in life. It's not simply a byproduct of our failure. It's not a symptom of stupidity or low intelligence. It's a vital step in the process of transformation. It rips us out of our usual habits of thinking and behaving and forces us to ask questions we wouldn't normally ask. It forces us to go places we wouldn't normally visit. Confusion pushes us to step out of our comfort zones to discover something that has been missing from our understanding. It comes just before a breakthrough, right when we discover something new—something that transforms us and expands us past our current set of limitations.

When we experience pain during life changes, it's not because the change itself is painful. Most change is needed and comes naturally based on our speed of inner growth. It's our resistance to the change that brings about discomfort, suffering, and conflicts. We often want to keep the familiar, regardless of how unhealthy it might be for us. What if you simply trusted the process and believed that better things lie ahead? What if you knew that the changes were going to result in your most coveted desires? What if this change was going to lead you where you've always wanted to go but it simply looks different than you expected? What if everything was happening exactly as it should? Go with it and find out.

You are a human being. As hard as it is to remember that sometimes, it's important to remind ourselves when we are in the midst of pain and heartache. As a human being, you are a *feeling* being. You feel your way through this world and not everything feels good. Not everyone is going to offer you reasons to celebrate or reasons to feel elated. It's not because you're a bad human being. It's not because you don't deserve to celebrate or to feel elated. It's because this world is full of different paths and people who are on their own journeys. They are feeling beings, as well, and they are simply trying to navigate this life just as you are. We don't always get it right, but it's important to not use our feelings or anyone else's feelings as the reason why we got it wrong. Nothing you feel is wrong. It's all perfectly appropriate given the precise circumstances and environment you find yourself in. Of course you would feel that way. That's how feeling beings feel when they bump up against the many experiences this world has to offer. Don't think of it as weakness, and don't punish yourself for it. Honoring your feelings is another way of honoring yourself.

When looking at an acorn, it's hard to imagine that one day it will grow to be a huge oak tree, nonetheless an entire forest. But everything it can become in the future is contained within itself right now. It simply grows a little bit at a time each day. When there is some sunshine, some water, it flourishes. Regardless of how small we feel today, all we need is a little bit of daily motivation and self-compassion to blossom into a bountiful being with many gifts. As we share our gifts and pass them on to others, we help them to become just as bountiful. The cycle continues until we are no longer just an acorn or a tree. Then, we are a forest.

What if you offered your body love instead of criticism? What if you offered it some compassion instead of insults? What if you saw the decades of abuse, wear-and-tear, and aging as cause for more love instead of less? What if you acknowledged the thousands of miles it has trekked through this rough and wild world and you felt nothing but appreciation and love for all it has withstood for you? What if you offered it more sleep, more hot baths, better foods, healthy exercise, fun activities, and more rest? What if you gave it more love? What if you stopped punishing it for belonging to you?

The following paragraph will offer you the apology you never received. It's up to you whether you want to accept it in the place of the one you didn't get. It's up to you whether you are now willing to let go and release the hold that the lack of apology has had on your wellbeing.

I'm sorry. I'm sorry for not being kind to you. You didn't deserve my careless words and thoughtless actions. I'm sorry I wasn't there for you when you needed me the most because I was only thinking of myself. I'm sorry for hurting you. I'm sorry for any damage I may have caused in your life. I'm sorry I wasn't able to see what a loving and deserving person you are. I'm sorry for my shortcomings. I'm sorry I didn't know better. I'm sorry I didn't know how to love you the way you deserved to be loved. I'm sorry for not being able to give you what you needed. I'm sorry for the way things ended between us. Most importantly, I'm sorry for not being able to say I'm sorry. I hope that you'll forgive me anyway. Not for me, but for yourself. I may not deserve your forgiveness, but you deserve the freedom.

Regardless of what you have been through or where you're going, I hope you're still able to soar to newer heights. I hope you find what you're looking for whether it's in faraway lands or at the base of your feet. I hope you find your joy again and laugh so hard your stomach muscles ache for days. I hope you keep the company of good friends and lovers who are worthy of your radiance. I hope you are finally able to reach that deep inner peace hidden within your bones. Most importantly, I hope you find yourself. And when you do, I hope you find that you were always a miraculous and spectacular being, worthy of the greatest love and the deepest peace. I honor you in hopes that you will one day learn to honor yourself.

The great thing about you is that you're still here. You made it through many stormy seas and you're still ready to get back in the boat. You're still brave enough to hope. You're still courageous enough to love. You still give of yourself with the same warmth you did before others tried to extinguish your flame. You're still filled with kindness even though the world hasn't given you much to be kind about. You're still open to great adventures and deep emotions. You're still here. You're still living. You're still you. How great it is that you're still you.

As you learn to quiet the chatter of your mind, as you release the stresses and worries of the outside world, as you silence the incessant noise of other people's thoughts and opinions, as you connect to the depths of your being and allow what's there to come forth, you will find a deep peace you have never known before. It will wash over you like the waves of the ocean and expand your chest like an exploding supernova. You will come into your own and discover what it really means to be you. You will be immersed in a love you have never felt before, and you will feel the totality of all that you are. Then, you will wonder why you ever tolerated anything less than the total and complete alignment of your being.

Soothing and Empowering "I" Statements:

It's a new morning and a new day. I can choose to feel ease today. And if I don't feel ease today, I can choose to find relief from what stresses me. Relief is something I can choose over and over again. I now know how.

Each new day is a new beginning. My experiences are getting better and better because each day, I feel better and better. The more ease I feel, the more peace I feel.

I trust that the right experiences will meet me today. I want to have fun with others. I want to laugh and feel more joy. I know more of these experiences are coming to me, and I eagerly anticipate them.

I feel better right now. I feel more ease in my body. I feel more relief. I feel more peace.

I am feeling more ease now. I can feel the difference in my body. I can feel my muscles relaxing and letting go of the tension. I can feel my chest expanding out with each calming breath. I can feel the heavy weight falling off of my relaxed shoulders. With each inhale and exhale, I can feel my body sinking deeper and deeper into relaxation.

I am learning balance in both body and mind. I am learning how to let go of things that no longer serve me. I am learning more about my body and how it functions in times of stress. I am learning how to speak its language and sooth its aches.

I know things are going to get better because they always do. Even when the worst thing happens and it hurts for a while, I still bounce back from it. I still wake up, I still eat my breakfast, I still live my life. There's no reason to believe that I won't get through this, too.

I trust my process. It is always leading me to my desired destination. The path might not look as I expect, but I trust that I am on my way and I will get there.

I accept my past and am open to seeing it from a better perspective. I am open to accepting that it was exactly what I needed at the time so that I can become who I want to become. I am open to accept that who I used to be played a huge role in who I'm now becoming. I don't have to hate my past self, and I don't have to hate my past experiences. It's all a journey. I accept all parts of me, including who I used to be.

I trust myself to get through this because I've gotten through everything so far. There's no reason for me to believe that I can't do it again. I've learned a lot of lessons and am smarter now than I have ever been before.

It's okay that I am where I am. I don't need to rush everything. There have been times when I tried to rush something and it didn't work out in my favor. There have been times when things took longer and it worked out best for me. I can trust in good timing, and I can stop trying to force it. I'll happen when it's ready.

I don't have to have all the answers. No one does. Some people know more than me on certain subjects, and I know more than them on other subjects. But no one knows everything. It's okay if I make decisions from partial knowledge; we all do. I can always adjust my choices as more information is revealed to me.

I'm learning as I go along. I know more today than I did yesterday. I am the smartest I have ever been. I am the strongest I have ever been. I am my best self right now, even when I feel tired or depressed. Mental and emotional progress can't be undone, so whatever it is I'm going through, it can't take away my growth.

I'm not behind on anything. I'm taking my time to figure out what works for me. I don't have to rush into anything and make choices quickly just because others have. I'm not other people, and they are not me.

This will pass just as everything else has passed. There were times when I thought I would never be able to get past an embarrassment or heartache, and yet I did. I've learned that everything can heal and I am open to healing.

There's nothing wrong with where I am. There's nothing wrong with what I have. There's nothing wrong with my growth or progress. Other people don't get to decide where I should be or how I should be. I get to decide that, and I'm deciding that there's nothing wrong with any of it.

Everyone has off days. Everyone has bad days. Everyone experiences sadness and anger and exhaustion. I'm going to give myself some time and care to bounce back from this, and I'm not going to shame myself for having the kind of day that everyone else has, as well.

No matter what I've done or not done, I am worthy of love. No matter what I've said or not said, I am worthy of love. No matter who I am or who I am not, I am worthy of love. No matter what I look like or don't look like, I am worthy of love. No matter what I weigh or don't weigh, I am worthy of love. No matter what, I'm worthy of love.

I accept my emotions as they come. I will no longer shame myself for having the same emotions other people have. I will no longer mentally abuse myself for being human. Everything I feel is normal and will pass eventually. It's okay to feel.

I accept my body as my own. It's okay for me to stay in it. It's okay for me to feel its sensations and aches. It's okay for anxiety and upset to arise because it will calm soon afterward. I don't have to run away or disconnect from anything happening in my body. I am safe in here.

It's okay for me to make decisions. I am free to choose what I believe is the best choice in this moment. If I later discover that it wasn't the best choice, I can always make another choice that's better. No matter what I choose, everything will be okay.

I can always find help if I need any. There is so much knowledge and experience all around me. People are so helpful and willing to share what they know. We might not have the same experiences, but they always have something new to teach me or offer me.

I'm finding more ease in making decisions. The more I allow myself the freedom to make mistakes, the less I make them. When I feel better, I do better.

I am in the process of accepting myself completely. I am learning to love myself completely. I understand that it's a process and it won't happen overnight, but I'm committed to being kinder to myself because I know that's where unconditional love begins.

I can find ten or fifteen different answers for every topic I bring up. When I allow myself to explore other people's thinking, I can find answers in places I never imagined. I'm open and willing to examine new thoughts about subjects I feel stuck in. I know others can offer me pathways I haven't considered.

There is a wealth of opportunity in each person I meet. They can offer me kindness, knowledge, connection, love, friendship, success, a good laugh. Each person is a new world that has been opened up to me. I gladly welcome them into my experience.

There are many people around me who want the best for me. They might have their own ideas about what's best for me, but their intentions are for me to have my best life.

I can feel my body relaxing and finding ease as I read these words. I can feel the difference in my breath, my stomach, my chest, my head. I can feel the tension melting away as ease returns. My body is finding its balance again.

I love knowing that the human body is capable of finding its balance simply by introducing a new thought. I love that I have more control over my mind and body than I had previously known. I love that I can now play with this until I get in the habit of ease and relaxation.

It's okay if I feel stressed every once in a while. Stress is a normal bodily reaction, and I can let it happen and then let it go. Stress doesn't mean I failed; it means there's another aspect of my life that needs some attention, love, and easing. I can do that.

My needs matter. My time matters. My energy matters. My feelings matter. My thoughts matter. What I do matters. Who I am matters.

I am worth healing. I am worth the time. I am worth the energy. I am worth the miracle. I deserve to be here. I am worthy of this life.

The right kind of support comes to me at the right time. Just when I think I can't handle something on my own, I receive support from others. I am reminded that I am not alone, that I am loved, and that people care about me.

I am in the process of learning how to be more of myself. I am learning how to express myself more freely and authentically. I am growing into my freedom.

My body knows how to heal and balance itself. My healing is already in progress. All I have to do is think thoughts that feel good and put myself in a state of ease. My body will take care of the rest.

I'm learning to trust my inner wisdom. Deep down inside, I know the right answers. I know what's right for me, and I'm choosing to listen to myself more.

As I go about my daily activities, I am paying closer attention to my body and needs. I now understand what helps my body remain in balance, and I am committed to providing more opportunities for relaxation and comfort.

I'm ready to let go of the things that no longer help or support me in my new intention for wellness and relief.

I'm ready to accept all that I am and all that I feel. I am open to accepting myself and allowing the healing of self-love and self-compassion. I understand that authenticity feels better than pretense, and I am now coming home to myself.

I am open to the right path for me. I am willing to let go of my old habits of stress and resistance. I am learning how to be in a more accepting and allowing state. I am learning the power of release.

I am giving myself the gift of forgiveness. I will no longer participate in self-abuse or harsh criticism over normal human processes. I am allowed to learn, explore, and grow.

I am open to feeling fulfilled in what I do. I am setting myself free from self-inflicted burdens and obligations. My first obligation is to my health and wellbeing. Without that, nothing else is possible.

All power exists in the present moment. There's nothing I can do about the past. All I can do for the future is to feel good now. The future is nothing more than a bunch of nows. If I feel good now, and now, and now, and now, then the future becomes filled with more feeling good.

It's important that I feel good. I'm acknowledging that now more than ever. I understand that now more than ever. I'm making it a priority to take better care of myself.

Every moment holds the possibility of peace, ease, and relaxation. It's a choice I make every day, and I am now more open to it.

I am willing to let go of what no longer works in my life. I am willing to release the power old mistakes had over me. I am open to all the new changes that are happening in my life. I am safe.

I am creating a new habit of thinking better feeling thoughts. I am in the process of creating better habits that keep me healthy and safe. The more I practice them, the easier they become.

I have power of the thoughts I think. I don't have to keep thinking thoughts that keep me afraid or angry. I am in the process of taking my power back as I become more deliberate with my thinking.

Who I am now is much wiser and stronger than I have ever been. Everything I have experienced has bettered me. I am still learning and growing. I am in the process of becoming.

There is always another way to look at the same situation. When my perception changes, the situation no longer feels the same. It changes because my thinking has changed. I am open to changing my mind.

I am open to seeing myself through more compassionate eyes. I deserve kindness from others and from myself. I am kind.

I create my future through the choices I make today. The choices I make today depend on the thoughts I think right now. I am choosing to think better feeling thoughts. I am choosing to change my future by feeling good right now.

The only limits that exist are in my thinking. I am open to thinking new thoughts and allowing new pathways to reveal themselves to me.

I trust that everything that crosses my path is there to benefit me in some way, shape, or form. I will learn something new from it. I will gain a better understanding about myself. It will make me stronger or smarter. It will be a clarifying experience.

I recognize that every experience is an opportunity and I can choose to gain something valuable from each one.

Today is a new day, and it will be what I choose to make of it. I am the one who chooses how I feel about today, how I feel about this moment, and how I feel about myself. I choose to feel good about where I am. My point of power is now and now is a great time to begin.

I lovingly let go of those who need to move on and find other experiences along their path. I release them and wish them well.

I trust that the people I love are experiencing whatever they need for the growth of their mind and spirit. I don't have to know what it is or how it comes about. I will offer my love and support but will let go of the need to control any circumstances. I trust that everything happens for their benefit. Even if I can't see it.

When I am ready to move on to the next stage in my life, career, or relationship, opportunities will be presented to me to take me there. I trust the timing of my life.

I am doing the best I can in this moment. As I experience new things, I grow more. As I learn more, I do better. Life presents me with the opportunities that will help me become the best version of myself.

I am open and receptive to new opportunities and experiences. I trust that they will lead me to where I need to be. I am stepping into my power and stepping out into the world.

I listen to my body with compassion. I give my body what it needs. I offer myself love, support, and kindness. I offer myself more ease and relaxation. I am feeling more ease right now.

I am giving myself permission to rest. I am giving myself permission to not know all the answers. I am giving myself permission to be as I am right here, right now.

There's something good to be found in every situation, regardless of how bad it might seem in the present moment. I am open to seeing the best in others and in myself. I am open to seeing the good in every situation.

I am ready to see that everything in my life happens for my benefit, even if I don't realize it in the moment. I am ready to allow the good around me into my awareness. I am open.

The more I relax, the more I see that everything eventually works out for my benefit. There's nothing wrong here. We're all trying the best we can. It's okay if we stumble every once in a while during the process.

I understand that when I was younger, I didn't know as much as I know now and I had much to learn. I understand that I made the choices I made because I didn't know better. I also understand that I still have much to learn and it's okay if I make choices that don't yield the best results. I am always learning.

I am open and receptive to allowing new avenues of income, new friends, and new experiences. I am open to the richness of life and all the gifts it has to offer me.

My life becomes easier as I become more allowing and receptive. The more open I am to new experiences, the less stress I feel.

I trust that the answers will come to me in the right moment. I don't need to struggle for them, and I don't have to justify the gifts I receive through pain or hard work. It's okay for me to receive simply because I am deserving. I don't need to earn the good things in my life. I accept it, and I deserve it.

Life is as good or as bad as I make it. If I allow the negative to get to me, then I'll have more negative experiences. If I allow myself to experience the positive without questioning it or being suspicious of it, then I'll experience more of it. I get to choose which one I feed. The power of my experience is in my hands.

I happily express my creativity. I accept that everyone is creative in their own unique way, and so am I. I enjoy the process of creating, and I enjoy the process of connecting. It's safe for me to express myself in creative and unique ways.

I am open to more opportunities for play. I enjoy having fun and am receptive to new experiences of fun.

I am ready for more enjoyable experiences. I am ready to enjoy every bite of food I eat. I am ready to enjoy every warm bath I soak in. I am ready to enjoy the sweet sound of every song I hear. I am ready to enjoy every aspect of my life as it is right now while I eagerly await more.

I am in the process of beneficial changes. Some I see, and others I haven't yet realized. Some I initiate myself, and others I allow into my experience. Either way, I am moving forward in a healthy direction.

I am thankful for the present moment because my point of power is always here. I get to choose where I go from here and which emotional state I will use as my means of transportation.

My emotions come and go, but what remains is my firm belief in my ability to become a healthy, successful, and joyous person. It doesn't matter if I feel upset one day or sad another. Eventually, those feelings pass and I advance forward, regardless of them.

I feel very hopeful about where I am right now in my life. I know that things can improve in a short period of time. I look forward to the wonderful experiences that are headed my way.

As I begin each day, I am going to look for things that please me and bring me joy. I'm going to notice the positive things more, and I'm going to allow myself to feel peace in them.

As I end each day, I'm going to feel appreciation for each experience that brought me fun, joy, or laughter.

My days are getting better and better, and I know it's because of all the work I'm doing in bringing myself relief and ease.

Amazing experiences are coming my way. I can feel it. I can feel my life shifting just by how I feel in my body. I can feel that the work I do on myself is creating the results I want. I can feel that it's all coming together perfectly.

All is well in my world.

PART 3
EXERCISES

Relief Exercises:

Simple and Easy

The following simple and common exercises were included based on their efficiency in helping the nervous system find or stay in balance, calm, and relaxation. Most of the exercises are effective in relieving stress and are backed by studies from Harvard, Columbia, UCLA, and many other universities and institutions.

You don't have to do all of the exercises to feel results. I've included a variety of them so there is something for everyone. Please choose those that feel good to you.

Most are exercises you probably do already. If that's the case, continue doing them and consider adding a few more. Switching up exercises can also help keep it fun and exciting. It's up to you on how you want to proceed and which you want to try. Keep it fun, and don't worry too much about whether you're doing it right or wrong.

The best way to gauge your results is how you feel. Do you feel more relief in doing the exercise? Then it's working for you. If you find it stressful, anxiety inducing, or frustrating, then skip that one. It's all about doing things that offer you relief.

Let's get started …

Relief Exercise: Breathe deeply. Breathing deeply from the belly stimulates the vagus nerve and offers immediate physical relief. If you're feeling frustrated or upset right now, take a moment and focus on your breathing. How is your breath? Is it shallow, short, or fast? Take a deep breath from your belly, extending it out, hold it for four seconds, and then release your breath, pulling your belly back in. Exhale longer than you inhale. Do this about five times, and you will trigger calm in your body.

Relief Exercise: Tense and release. In moments of stress and anger, our bodies naturally tense up to prepare for a possible physical altercation or so we can run away from danger. This is a simple exercise to help discharge pent up aggression in the body from unresolved stress and anger. Start with the bottom part of your body and slowly move up. Tighten your feet muscles. Squeeze and hold them for 10-15 seconds. Then, release them. Feel the relief in letting go. Sit with that feeling for about 10-15 seconds. Then, move up to your calves, then your thighs, your stomach, your hands, etc. Take about 10-15 minutes to go through your entire body. As you release, you will feel the tension melting away.

Relief Exercise: Laugh. Laughing has a very powerful affect on your body. It uplifts your mood by lowering the stress hormone cortisol and increasing the happy chemicals dopamine and endorphins. For stress relief, put on a funny movie or show and laugh for a few minutes. Call up a friend who always makes you laugh. Recall a funny event or memory. Laughing for a few minutes a day can positively change the chemicals and hormones in your body.

Relief Exercise: Play. As we get older, we stop doing the things that naturally allowed us to relieve stress as children. We think growing up means we have to be stressed, as if it's a requirement to being an adult. Stress might mature us, but play heals us. One of the fastest ways to reduce stress is to play. The act of playing can improve mood, increase joy, and reduce stress. Whether you're playing a sport, a game, or just goofing off with your friends, playfulness benefits your mental wellbeing and builds your resilience toward future stressors. You may have grown up, but that doesn't mean you have to stop playing.

Relief Exercise: Listen to calming music. Studies show that listening to relaxing or calming music can lower blood pressure and reduce anxiety. However, don't listen to sad or depressing music because it will put your body into a more resigned state as opposed to a relaxed one. You can also listen to nature sounds. Research also shows that spending some quality time in nature can greatly reduce stress. However, if you're nowhere near nature, listening to nature sounds can have a similar effect. There are many nature sound apps and videos online that you can use to set the tone of your mood and bring calm to your body.

Relief Exercise: Push against a wall. Stand in front of a wall leaving less than an arms length between you and the wall. Place your arms on the wall, and push against it as if you're trying to move it back. Keep your elbows bent a bit; don't stiffen your arms. Push and feel the tenseness of your arm muscles, your leg muscles, and your stomach/core muscles as you push. Push for a few seconds, then release. Feel the relief in your body as you let go. Take some deep breaths, and feel the ease returning to your body. Notice what emotions came up as you engaged your muscles. Did you feel angry, sad, upset? Repeat the exercise if needed until you feel complete relief.

Relief Exercise: Float. According to a study published in the International Journal of Stress Management, floating in water activates the body's relaxation response and helps lower stress-hormone levels. Almost 80% of the subjects from the Swedish study showed improvements in mood and muscle tensions. Some even reported that they were less depressed. If you have access to a pool or other body of water, practice floating.

Relief Exercise: Notice life more. If your connection to the world is only through the TV or the Internet, then you are only going to hear about the most sensationalized events. The news will report on the one tragic accident as opposed to the millions of cars that made it to their destinations safely. They'll report on the one home invasion robbery rather than the millions of homes that are safe and well. The news will never tell you that the Johnson family had a wonderful meal together and fell asleep on the couch watching a family movie. They'll only tell you about the Johnson family if someone is killed or kidnapped. The news skews our perspective of the world by picking out a few events that shock us and feed on our fears. Look around your neighborhood right now; look around your office. What's happening? You'll find people eating dinner, reading, playing with kids, enjoying time alone. The normal boring stuff we take for granted every day. That's life, too. We don't notice it because it's not dramatic enough to grab our attention. Take a few moments in your day to notice everyday life. Notice the gardener, notice the woman on the bench reading a book, notice the car pulling into the driveway safely. Notice everyday life. It's good. It's well. It's safe. Breathe it in.

Relief Exercise: Chant. Recently, it was discovered that chanting the "om" sound stimulates the vagus nerve. Trauma expert Dr. Peter Levine recommends doing a "voooo" chant.

However, both sounds create a vibration in your throat and in your belly/gut, so you can choose either one. The vibration from the sound stimulates the vagus nerve, which activates your parasympathetic nervous system, causing a calming affect in your mind and body. If you can feel your gut vibrating as you hold the sound, know that it's working. Take a few minutes, sit somewhere quiet, and chant either om or voooo. Breathe in deep and slowly, let out the sound as you exhale. Pay attention to the vibrations in your stomach and gut as you do it. Then, take another deep breath and let it out again. Chanting for 3-5 minutes can create immediate calm. You're welcome to do it longer if you enjoy it.

Relief Exercise: Watch fish swim. A recent study by the National Marine Aquarium in the UK has shown that watching fish swim in an aquarium can lower heart rate and high blood pressure by creating a calming Zen effect in the mind. Whether it's the natural flow of movement, the refreshing colors, or the water, looking at an aquarium can create a calming atmosphere both in the home and in the mind.

Relief Exercise: Dance. Take fifteen or twenty minutes, put on three or four fun, upbeat songs, and dance your heart out. When your heart rate accelerates, your body releases endorphins, which help you to relax and feel good. Dancing increases your mood and confidence. Even if you're dancing alone in your room, you'll be able to take the positive effects with you everywhere. Make it a habit to dance at least 3 times a week, even if it's to just one song.

Relief Exercise: Sing. Singing is really a form of guided breathing. Moreover, when that guided breathing is combined with the vibrations from the vocal chords, it stimulates the vagus nerve. The act of singing or humming has a biological soothing effect on the body, which has been shown to benefit cardiovascular and respiratory functions. In other words, singing is good for your mood, heart, and lungs.

Relief Exercise: Cut down on social media. Studies have shown that social media actually makes us unhappy. When we watch our friends go on vacations, party, or have fun, it depresses us about our own lives. Even though they're momentary snippets of their lives, we tend to compare it to our own lives and feel negatively about ourselves. Social media is also full of negative news stories about how terrible human beings are or how bad things are in the world. Cutting down on social media can reduce a lot of stress.

Relief Exercise: Strengthen social connections. This exercise refers to the social connections we have outside of social media. While you can still speak with friends online, there's a different level of intimacy and bond with having face-to-face conversations and connections. People who have friends they can count on during times of stress experience less stress than those who keep their emotions to themselves. Strong social connections promote mental wellbeing and balance. It's important to have avenues of healthy expression, and having friends you can trust with your emotions is a powerful way to strengthen your resilience toward future stress. Healthy social connections make us feel connected, heard, validated, and relieved.

Relief Exercise: Recall a positive decision, behavior, or action. When you're in the middle of stressing about a choice you need to make or a perceived mistake you already made, stop for a moment and recall a memory where you made the right choice. Remind yourself that we all do the best we can with the information we have in this moment. It's okay if our choices don't yield our exact intentions; no one has that precision and accuracy. Look at your current situation through a more balanced perspective. You will make good decisions and not-so-good decisions. So do others. It's a normal and natural process of life. It just means you're human.

Relief Exercise: Increase physical touch. Out of the five human senses, touch is the first to develop in an infant. Babies who are touched more develop a stronger immune system and a healthier nervous system. Some studies even suggest that massage can speed up weight gain in premature babies. Human contact and physical touch are necessities to our emotional and mental wellbeing. Whether you get a massage from a professional, have your partner increase their physical affection, or talk a close friend into longer hugs, increasing physical touch from another human being can relieve stress and trigger the parasympathetic nervous system.

Relief Exercise: Practice walking meditation. Walking meditation isn't simply going for a walk outside—because usually when we do that, we spend the whole time worrying and stressing about everything. In this exercise, you pay attention to the world around you. You make a conscious effort to pick out a particular smell, color, sight, sound, and texture in your environment to focus on. Touch a flower and feel its texture. Is it soft, is it rough? Staying in the present experience can help reduce stress in your body.

Relief Exercise: Look outside a window. When the chaos of the world overwhelms you, take a look outside. What do you see? Where are you? If you see the city, if you see traffic, simply look at the flow of the cars moving. It's full of people going to their destinations. People who want peace. People who want happiness. People who want to be safe. People just like you. Really watch what is happening. If you see nature, keep looking around at all the peace. Watch the trees sway and the birds fly. Take a moment and take in what is happening right now.

Relief Exercise: Stay curious. The nervous system is unable to be curious and anxious at the same time. They are mutually exclusive emotions. Curiosity says, "My environment is interesting and I want to explore." Anxiety says, "My environment is dangerous, and I must run or fight to stay alive." By engaging our curiosity, we relieve the stress and anxiety we feel in our bodies. Find something in your environment that you feel curious about. Explore it. Use your senses, touch it or examine it further with your eyes. Do you notice something different, something new? Can you feel curious about a new subject? A new person in your life? Increase your curiosity, and it will naturally decrease your stress and anxiety.

Relief Exercise: Reduce technology. Set aside some time where you can turn off your phone, TV, and computer and do something that doesn't involve technology. We've become addicted to our phones and tablets. We lose ourselves in the chatter of the Internet and overwork our minds. Add one activity you can do a day that doesn't involve technology, and reduce about thirty minutes of TV or Internet time. Do something that engages your physical environment instead of the virtual one.

Relief Exercise: Spend time in nature. Nature possesses both a healing and a calming quality. Walking through the woods, sitting by the beach, or simply spending time in a park can greatly reduce stress levels. Spending time in a natural atmosphere can recharge our batteries as well as relax our nervous systems. Listening to nature sounds, like birds singing, the crashing of the ocean waves, pouring rain, or trees swaying in the wind, can produce a meditative effect on the body and mind. If you are unable to go to nature, you can put on nature sounds, close your eyes, and imagine yourself there. It won't have the same exact effect, but it's a good alternative.

Relief Exercise: Practice gratitude. Making a list of 3-5 things you feel grateful for daily can significantly improve your overall mood and reduce stress. It doesn't have to include the major aspects of your life, as in your kids or house. It can be the hot chocolate you enjoyed in the morning. It can be the twenty minutes of silence and peace you had in the afternoon.

It can be the beautiful birds outside your window. The more you practice this exercise, the more you rewire your brain. This sets up the habit of looking for positive things in your life, as opposed to mostly noticing what isn't going right. You'll become more conscious of what you enjoy in your daily experience.

Relief Exercise: Meditate. There is so much research now on the benefits of meditation to the body and mind. It rewires your brain and creates measurable and observable effects in the body. People who meditate regularly have better focus, memory retention, a calmer mind, lower blood pressure, and a healthier heart rate. It has a two-fold effect on the body and mind. Meditating for about 15-20 minutes a day three times a week can change your brain and make it resilient against stress. If it's too difficult to begin with 15 minutes, you can start with 3-5 minutes and build up each week.

Relief Exercise: Do some yoga. Yoga, to put it simply, is the act of stretching while breathing into your body. However, it's so much more than that. It creates a powerful healing and balancing effect in the body. Yoga increases the production of nerve cells, boosts your immune system, helps you focus, decreases chronic pain and depression, increases blood flow and oxygenates the blood, triggers the parasympathetic nervous system, strengthens your vagal tone, and builds resilience against stress. Not only does yoga relieve stress, but it also helps your body become more effective in preventing future stress. It's beneficial to just about every organ in your body as well as your muscles, nerves, cells, and even your bones. There is no part of you that won't benefit from doing yoga.

Relief Exercise: Do something physical. Getting physical with your body can help you release pent-up stress and find more ease. Hitting or kicking the gym bag can allow the charged-up, stuck energy to finally be released from your muscles. We tend to stay tense throughout the day, stiffening our muscles and creating fatigue in our bodies. This leaves us tired all the time. To release that tension, some require a nice massage and others require a good punch or kick.

Relief Exercise: Run. Our ancestors, when faced with stress, either ran away or stayed and fought. This innate reaction to stress is still active in us, even though their stressors were animal predators and ours are traffic and an angry boss or spouse. Your body doesn't know the difference; it just knows it feels stress. It's hardwired to move in some way, shape, or form when it's stressed. It feels natural for your body to run when it feels stressed. Consider taking a jog around the block, or jump on a treadmill for a few minutes. A good run can help clear your mind and body.

Relief Exercise: Aromatherapy. Our sense of smell is a powerful memory activator and mood changer. Simply by smelling the natural oils of flowers, roots, and other parts of a plant, we can enhance our sense of relaxation and improve our moods. Lavender, chamomile, and jasmine have been shown to reduce stress. Peppermint and rosemary have been shown to help boost memory retention. Whether you're looking for mood stabilizers, stress relief, self-esteem boosters, or an aphrodisiac, aromatherapy can help.

Relief Exercise: Get creative. Human beings are naturally creative. Everyone as a child loves arts, crafts, and coloring books. Children sing, dance, and draw. It doesn't matter to them that they aren't very good at it. Good and bad is not the point—the activity is. Creativity reduces stress because it forces the mind to become present in an activity that engages different parts of the brain from the one that worries or feels fear. It's up to you to find which creative activity works for you. Some might relax you; others might frustrate you. Only you will know which one works. Try drawing, painting, coloring, singing, dancing, needlepoint, sculpting, or any other kind of artistic craft. Try building something, or just get your hands dirty in paint. It doesn't have to be good. It only has to induce the feeling of fun or relaxation.

Relief Exercise: Play with a pet. Animals are great stress reducers. Owning a pet has been scientifically proven to reduce high blood pressure, relieve anxiety, and help with depression and feelings of isolation. Petting animals can increase levels of oxytocin, which is a stress-reducing hormone, and it can decrease production of cortisol, which is a stress-inducing hormone. Animals also force you to become more active, which is also beneficial to reducing stress. The next time you feel stressed or frustrated, take your dog for a walk or play with your cat. It will help both of you.

Relief Exercise: Journal. Take a few minutes out of your day to journal your thoughts. Sometimes, seeing it on paper brings you more clarity; other times, it helps you release it and let it go. If you are feeling angry, sad, or frustrated, it helps to write it out and then read it over. In the process of writing it out, you are letting go. In the process of reading it over, you are gaining clarity because you feel differently after writing it out. This helps you shift your perspective a bit, and you might find some answers. Or you might find that it's not as bad as you first believed. Journaling can help you realize that your problems don't feel as big or bad once some time has passed. As you look back at the things that frustrated you, you will begin to see that momentary stressors aren't as terrible as you first imagined them to be. Some time and distance helps put things in perspective. The more you do this, the more you will be able to apply it to your current stressors. You will remember that it's probably not as bad as you think it is, and that will help you relax even more.

Relief Exercise: Hug more. Hugs have been shown to improve mood, lower blood pressure, stabilize heart rate, and reduce anxiety. Hugging releases the bonding chemical oxytocin, which reduces stress hormones. It's also known as the trust chemical because it increases the feeling of trust in others. When you first greet or say goodbye to your friends, children, or other family members, give them a warm hug. Hold it for as long as it's comfortable, and if it's appropriate, rub their back with your hand. It's healthy for both of you.

Relief Exercise: Cold water. Splash cold water on your face, or take a cold shower. Cold triggers your vagus nerve, which stimulates the relaxation part of your nervous system. Some studies have shown that if you immerse your face in cold water immediately after exercising, it can instantly accelerate the parasympathetic reactivation response through the vagus nerve. This will turn on your immune system, reduce your heart rate, and stimulate the motility of the intestines. It is also effective in activating the vagus nerve, even if you haven't exercised.

Relief Exercise: Shower. Take a warm shower and concentrate on how the water feels against your skin. Focus on the sensations in your body. Become present in the act of taking a shower. Feel the warm water cascading down your head, down your face, down your neck, your chest, your stomach, your legs, and your feet. Feel it massaging your body as it cleanses away your stress, anxiety, and frustrations. Imagine those negative feelings washing off of you and going down the drain. Tell yourself that you've just pushed your reset button and once you leave that shower, you are newly purified.

Relief Exercise: Have an orgasm. An orgasm triggers the parasympathetic nervous system, which immediately puts the body in a calm and relaxed state. Whether you're with someone else or by yourself, regularly having an orgasm can keep your body healthy, regulated, stress-free, and can even clear your acne. Scientists at the New England Research Institute in Massachusetts performed a study that showed that men who had sex/orgasms at least twice a week had a 50% lower chance of experiencing a heart attack. Orgasms can save your life.

Discharge Resistance Exercises:

The following pages focus on exercises that help you release resistance from your body. The first exercise on page 200 is most effective in releasing tension and resistance from stress. You can also use it if you have a negative response to positive statements and affirmations in this book.

Discharging

The body has its own language, its own rules, and its own way of doing things. The best way to access the language of the body is through the breath. Since the nervous system controls your breathing and heart rate in times of stress, that's what we're going to use as a tool to create relaxation within your body. We're going to talk to our body through our breathing. We're going to tell it to activate the parasympathetic nervous system and flood the body with relief and calm. We're going to sit with it as it releases what it needs to release so it can return to balance.

Two of the most powerful tools you have in your body are your focus and your breath. If you use them correctly, you can create a lot of ease, relief, regulation, and balance. And if you don't use them correctly, you can create a lot of tension, stress, uneasiness, and anxiety.

This might sound like a simple approach, but it's not when you have lived in stress and upset for many years. It might be a difficult process because it will be a process you're not used to. And it's going to take some time before you can create the habit of relaxation or master it completely.

On paper, it's simple because nervous system regulation is a simple process. It's the normal process of your body. It's something your nervous system is supposed to do easily. However, if you've been living with the habit of stress, then you will be tempted to resort back to that old protective habit.

If you do that, it's okay. Work on it slowly over time. It's a process, and that process takes time and practice. Don't judge or blame yourself for choosing stress. As long as you're aware that you're doing it, then that's progress.

We are going to learn to approach the body and its sensations through focused breathing, curiosity, and allowing.

Focused breathing isn't meditation in the traditional sense; it's mindfulness. It's a bit different in that it's about being mindful in your body as you're having an experience. You're not sitting down to breathe and then witnessing your breath. You're living your life and bringing your attention to your body as it tenses up in conversation, as you hold your breath while walking, as you become nauseated from fear in your boss's office. It's about living in your body as you live your life. It's about connecting with your experience instead of numbing yourself through stress. The brain-body connection is only a breath away.

The second step is about inquiry. It's about feeling more curious about what's happening in your body and less afraid or threatened by its sensations. It's about not judging the stress but looking into where it is and what it's doing there.

Curiosity will help you feel safe in exploration, while fear and judgment will make you shut down and disconnect to avoid pain and suffering. Curiosity will also help you stay in your body as you're having an experience. If you're asking, "Hmm what is this?" You're more likely to allow your focus to stay in your body and explore, as opposed to judging the sensation as harmful and then scaring yourself out of your bodily experience. Sometimes, we use stress as a means to cover up other emotions we would rather not feel. Sometimes, it's easier to feel stressed about the dishes than upset about how you were treated at work. We learn to numb our other emotions through chronic stress.

The feeling of curiosity, however, is like an antidote to the sympathetic nervous system's stressful response. When you are curious about your environment, you are not afraid of it. You are willing to look and explore and experience because curiosity feels safe and even fun. Approaching anything with a sense of interest and curiosity will put you in a more allowing state, both in your body and in your mind.

Once you feel safe enough through curiosity, then you can begin to allow your body to feel whatever it is feeling without adding additional stress, constriction, tension, or disconnection. You are allowing it to be what it is without adding negativity to it, which only feeds the stress. You are allowing it to pass through and release.

These three steps are the process of staying connected within your body and helping it become balanced. If you can practice this with sensations of stress, anxiety, sadness, and anger, you can help your body become more regulated.

To feel safe in your body, to feel at home with yourself, you have to feel in your body. You have to allow feelings to come up in your body without making it mean that you're sick or broken or wrong or weak. And if you do feel those things, allow yourself to feel them in your body too. Because when you say, "I'm weak," your body has a reaction, even if you don't notice it. You feel it in your stomach or head or chest. Your muscles tighten or your chest constricts. You might be so used to it that you don't even notice when it's happening. However, feelings always show up in the body. And if you want to reconnect with the deep peace within yourself, you have to allow the reconnection of your mind and body.

A part of allowing the reconnection is not judging the sensations that show up or the feelings that arise; it's about breathing and allowing them to be whatever it is that they are being. This will return them to a state of calm and balance. If we don't add judgment and shame to what we observe, then they pass. But once we judge what we feel, then we prolong negative feelings and create a stress loop.

Sit with the constriction in your chest, sit with the nausea in your stomach, sit with the pressure in your head. Let them be. Breathe into them. Don't be afraid of them. They are merely messengers from your body saying, "I want relief." And you provide relief by breathing and allowing your body to return to ease. If you judge, if you make them wrong, then you add more tension and stress, which is the opposite of the relief your body is asking for.

Since the mind has learned to numb in times of stress or negative emotion, the best course of action for regulation is body mindfulness. Stay in your body. When you stay in your body, it will return to regulation. It's when you leave it or resist it that you keep it in an incomplete cycle.

When you feel the stress, become conscious of how you're breathing. Stay with the frustration. Breathe through it. Pay attention to the feeling in your stomach. Where in your body does the stress show up? Muscles? Back? Head? Intestines? Take your focus there. Do this every time you are stressed, angry, or sad. You can even do it when you're joyful or excited. Notice where in your body your emotions show up frequently.

Notice the patterns. Your body is speaking to you. Listen to what it has to say. Notice what's happening without creating a story around it. Acknowledging the sensation is not the same as judging it. You're not making the sensation wrong, or bad, or off. You're just bringing your focus and attention to it and breathing into it. You're welcoming it and listening to what it has to say. You're letting it pass naturally.

It's not about pushing past the emotion or even rising above it. When we try to do that, the negative emotion digs in deeper. It keeps the cycle going, and we keep coming back to it. What you want to do is feel the emotion, go to the center of it, and then breathe into it. When you breathe into it, it dissolves.

It's critical to the regulation process that you stay in your body. It's important that you breathe through the experience. That you allow your body to have its natural reactions and responses. If you begin trembling, sweating, or your heart starts racing, remember that this is normal. Your body is supposed to respond that way, and nothing has gone wrong. It's important that during these situations, you bring your attention into your body.

Stay with your body as it has the experience. Allow it to automatically trigger the recovery process. Your breathing will return to normal, your chest will open up, your stomach will calm, and the trembling will ease. You will complete the nervous system process within a matter of minutes. You will return to balance so long as you don't interrupt the process or prolong it.

Body Mindfulness:

So let's say that you are going about your day and you have a stressful experience. You begin to feel tension in your body. Maybe you feel some fear or pain. Your body begins to react to your experience of the event. So what do you do first?

The moment when you notice the tension or the constriction of your muscles, take a deep breath and begin the body mindfulness process. Bring your focus and attention into the areas of your body where you feel the changes from stress.

Where do you feel the stress? Scan your body for symptoms. Do your leg muscles feel tight? Does your throat feel dry? Does your chest feel heavy? Stay with your body as it activates. Focus on one symptom at a time.

Describe the symptoms in your mind using shapes, sizes, and colors. Does it feel like there's a rock on your chest? What color is it? How big is it? Is it round or with jagged edges?

Focus on the feeling of the symptom and describe it as best you can. Then, take deep breaths into it and see what happens. Is the rock getting smaller? Is it getting lighter? Is it changing into something else? Are there any changes in how you feel? Do your hands suddenly get warmer? Does your breathing get more relaxed? Focus on each symptom and allow it to release as you describe it and breathe into it. This is how you discharge built-up stress/activation in your body.

If the tension is regarding a specific line like, "Everything always works out for me" or "I'm always safe" see if you can find where in your body you're resisting that statement. If you feel a knot in the pit of your stomach regarding, "I'm always safe." Then there's some old habitual body memory that is responding to the new intention. It's resisting because it's used to responding in a specific way to the feelings of not being safe. So if you try to introduce the opposite, it will create tension and trigger the old sensation and bodily reaction. Whatever comes up, breathe into it and let it go. It's okay to let go. It's okay to be safe. Focus your mind on the knot. Go through the descriptive process, and see what comes up. Breathe into it and let it unknot. Let it release.

Discharging is about focusing on, breathing into, and engaging the symptoms in the body by using the part of the brain that is creative, as opposed to afraid. Whether it's a current stressful event or a passage in a book that brings up resistance, this same process can help you in both instances.

When we breathe during stress, it's commonly in the chest. It's an upper body kind of breath. What you want to do instead is breathe from your diaphragm in your belly. Every time you take a breath, you want your belly to expand out and then sink back in when you release. Heavy and rapid chest breathing will make you nauseated or dizzy. To breathe right, to breathe in order to calm, you have to breathe from your belly. Long, calm, deep breaths.

Breathe into your tight muscles. Breathe into the tightness in your chest. Breathe into your headache. Keep your focus on those areas as you move it one by one, breathing into the sensations. Breathe into the pain. Breathe into the fear. Breathe into your body. Explore the sensations of your body through curiosity. What is this tension? What is this pain? Where am I feeling it? What feels tighter? How does my throat feel? Is it drier? Some people feel the sensation of choking when they become anxious or stressed. It almost feels as though someone has placed their hands around their throats. Notice that as well.

The first three places you want to take your attention are your throat, chest, and stomach. What comes up in those areas? Is it heavy? How does it feel? Is it tight? Breathe as you explore with your focus. Notice what's happening.

Acknowledge what you feel as you feel it. No matter what you feel. It doesn't have to be anger or sadness or a heavy emotion. It can be just feeling tired and annoyed. Maybe your feet hurt, which is a pretty clear indication of being tired. Then, acknowledge that. Don't push it away or ignore it. Don't numb the sensations away.

Sit somewhere quiet and breathe into your body. Breathe into your tiredness, your achy muscles, the pain in your feet. Breathe into the aching of your feet. Acknowledge that your body is tired and its asking for rest. Breathe and find relief, and then give your body rest. Take a deep breath and let your body know that you hear it, that you are listening to its needs, that you're paying attention to it, that you acknowledge what it needs. And that you will give it what it needs, whether it's rest or food or water or anything else.

It's also important to acknowledge what your mind is saying about the physical sensations of your body. Your feet are tired and maybe your mind is saying, "I'm always tired. I never get any rest. No one ever helps me." Acknowledge the mental chatter that comes up as you're having the physical sensations in your body.

We create meaning out of all of our experiences, and that's true for the pain we feel in our bodies, as well. It's important to breathe through the self-created meanings, too. It's important to let it say what it needs to say and acknowledge that, as well.

As soon as you read something that creates tension in your body, focus in your body. Where does the resistance show up? Where don't you believe you can be healthy or happy? Is it in your chest? Your stomach? Sit with that resistance. How old is it? Is it yours? Is it your mother's? Wherever you picked up that belief from doesn't matter as much as your ability to now let it go. Set it free. Breathe into the sensations of resistance and release it. Allow the resistance to dissipate. Feel the relief.

Ground Yourself:

Ground yourself to where you are. Where are you right now as you're reading this book? Stop for a moment and feel yourself in the room. Feel the chair/sofa/bed underneath you. How does it feel on your bottom or your back? Is it soft? Comfortable? Does it feel like you're sitting on a pillow or a rock? How do your feet feel on the ground? Can you feel how firm they're planted on the ground? Move your feet a bit, and feel the firmness of the ground.

Feel yourself standing where you're standing. Sitting where you're sitting. Feel the weight of your body anchoring you to the ground/chair.

The Book of Relief

Look around the room. Do you notice anything new or unusual? Are there paintings? Posters? If you're outside, look around the stores or streets. How many items can you spot that are blue? What about yellow? Engage your environment with your eyes and focus. I am here. I am safe. Nothing has gone wrong. I am safe in my body. How does that feel? Did it bring anything up? Did you feel relief or more tension reading that?

If you felt tension, ground yourself some more. Feel the seat beneath you. What are your feet doing? How does your body feel where it is? Where are your hands? What are they doing? Are they hot or cold? Get present to your body in the room. Look around the room some more. You are here.

You are okay. Yes, you might be tired or in pain, but overall, you are okay. You are safe where you are. Don't allow the stress or upset to take you out of the room. Instead of flying off in your mind and disassociating from the pain or disassociating from your current emotional experience, ground yourself to where you are by using your physical senses. Don't let your mind take you into some other scenario in which something terrible happens to you or someone you love. You're not there. You're here. Now.

Don't let your mind separate from your body or from the room. Stay here. Breathe in and breathe out. Keep yourself centered within your body and keep yourself grounded in the room. Look around the room. Can you find five items that are the color blue? How many round items can you find? Use your eyes. The eyes are the most powerful tool to keep you in the present. Just by orienting them around the room, you can shift your feelings instantly. Use them to keep yourself present.

Engaging your eyes in your environment has been shown to stop panic attacks and help regulate the nervous system. Since anxiety is all about what happened before or what might happen later, the most effective way to ease it is to become engaged with your current environment and reality. When you become present, your brain stops seeing the present moment through the past. The present moment is safe; it's the past that's on repeat in your mind and body.

Let yourself feel whatever it is you're feeling without judgment. Don't run away from it mentally. It's not as painful as you think it's going to be. Allowing yourself to sit with the pain and feel it completely is actually less painful than avoiding pain. As you allow your body to feel and be what it is, then you will begin to feel more calm and ease. All dis-ease stems from the body not being at ease. It's because we resist and numb our feelings and sensations. We don't sit with them. We don't give ourselves permission to feel.

Give yourself permission to feel. It's okay. You won't lose yourself in the pain. You won't. You will come out of it once your body is done with the process. Let it have its processes. Nothing is a permanent state. Every emotion passes as long as we don't numb ourselves. Let it come and let it go without making it mean anything other than that your body is having a sensation.

It's important that your nervous system finds relief. Learning to consciously calm yourself is the most effective way of reprogramming your brain and regulating your nervous system. Get present in your body when you're having an emotion. Don't judge it. Don't disassociate. Being angry doesn't mean you're a horrible person, or that you can't heal, or that you're doing it wrong. It doesn't mean anything in the present moment. It's a reaction. Sit with it for a moment.

Breathe into the emotion. Breathe into the anger. Breathe into the frustration. Breathe into the sadness. Just breathe. You have control over your breath and your focus. Bring your focus to your breath and then to your body. Connect mind and body, and let them do what they need to do to regulate and find balance.

Inquiry and Action:

Ask yourself, what am I feeling in the moment? Get very present with the feeling now. Once you have identified the emotion, ask yourself, where am I feeling it? Emotions always show up in your body. Is it a knot in your stomach? Dry throat? Headache? Find the feeling in your body. Does it feel like tense muscles? Shallow breathing? Get present within your body. Breathe into the sensations and get present to it. Stay present to the emotion as it shows up in your body. This is body connection.

Ask yourself, what would make me feel better? Is there an action you can take to ease the situation or yourself? Maybe it's just more breathing, maybe it's walking away from the problem, or maybe it's having an important conversation with someone.

As long as you breathe into your feeling and accept it in your body, the stress will pass. Once it passes, then you can take a proactive action that will benefit the situation further instead of causing more harm or damage.

Every time you have a default emotion, you're also going to have a default bodily reaction. Some of us have become numb to this process because we deny our emotions and cut the body/mind connection. However, they are always tied together. As you change your body's reaction to the emotion through mindful breathing, you will also begin to change your cognitive response to it.

Before, the anger emotion might have triggered a memory of another anger response and made you judge yourself based on the past. It might have made you label yourself in negative terms. As your cognitive response changes, so will the length of the emotion. Then, you will begin creating a new cycle between your body and mind.

Here's how it works: you have a strong emotion. You get present in your body, you breathe into it, you connect with it, you trigger physical calm in your nervous system. This then begins to trigger calming thoughts instead of angry or judgmental ones. This creates calm in your mind. So now you have a calm nervous system, calm thoughts, and calm emotions.

You don't do anything with the anger or the sadness. You don't act on it. You sit with it. You breathe into it. You inquire about it. You explore it. This is how you work on your emotional intelligence. Instead of fighting them, resisting them, or using them to create destruction in your life, you become curious about the feelings. As you learn more about your feelings and where they come from, it'll become easier to deal with other people and their emotions. You'll automatically search within instead of acting out. Then, once you're calm again, you can choose an appropriate action. Not an action that is inspired by anger or stress, but one that is inspired by your calm.

As you practice doing this, you will begin to regulate your nervous system and your mind. This will lead to calmer emotions and a stronger ability to deal with them. Your body will learn a positive and effective way to deal with stress. The next time you feel angry, you won't feel that level of stress in your body, you won't judge yourself harshly, and it won't last as long. This is how you begin the process of balance and peace.

Disidentify:

As you breathe into your body and allow the experience to pass, you disidentify with it. Instead of attaching meaning, making it personal, getting upset, creating tension, and triggering stress, you let it go. You do not identify with the experience. Instead, you let it pass through you because it's not you.

When you attach to the experience by making it personal, your mind and body become stuck in it. It becomes a part of you; it means you're a terrible mother, it means you don't know how to do anything right, it means you're bad at your job. It becomes a part of your identity. But a lot of that identity is a response to an inner imbalance created through chronic stress. And once you begin regulating, you'll learn to disidentify as well. It's a part of the process. You won't feel as responsible for every experience that comes your way.

You are not the anger. You are not the thing that's triggering the anger. You are not the meaning placed on your anger. The anger is simply your body's chemical reaction to an experience that you are judging to be personal about you. This is not who you are.

You are the ease and regulation of your body. You are the breath that expands and contracts in each moment. You are the balance and the peace. Focus yourself back in your body to the center of your being, and let it pass.

It will take some practice, but as you learn to do this you will feel much more peace and ease. You will feel the stress dissipating from your body. You won't be easily activated by people or events in the future. You'll find that you're not as bothered as you used to be. Your contraction periods will get less and less.

Regulation means that you will be present in your body and in your life. You will trust yourself to handle what the present moment has to offer you. As you practice handling each experience that comes your way, you will gain more confidence in your ability to handle more.

As you gain confidence, as you gain peace, as your body finds balance, you'll find yourself feeling less and less stress. Not because there are a lack of stressful events in your life but because you stopped seeing and feeling them as stressful. They take on new meaning and you respond differently. It creates a complete shift in your perspective.

Allow Contraction:

As you practice being in your body and allowing relaxation, you'll have periods of expansion and contraction. You'll have moments, days, or weeks where you will feel good and energetic and your chest will expand and you will feel as if you are in balance. You will feel brighter and life will feel easier.

Then you will have moments of contraction, where you'll be upset at your husband or mother. Someone will say something or do something and it'll trigger your deep inner shame, which will trigger your old survival methods, which will trigger the stress response again.

This is a part of the process. If you don't judge your contraction period, you'll pass through it. If you begin judging it, making yourself wrong, or adding to it, then you'll be stuck in the contraction period.

It doesn't mean that the healing isn't working. In fact, it means that it is working. That's how healing happens. It's like breathing. Expansion. Contraction. In. Out. This is how your whole being is breathing. Don't judge the out breath as being wrong or less important.

If negativity is coming up, breathe through it. Remember that it's just the contraction period. You are not a failure. You shouldn't feel ashamed for getting it wrong because it's not wrong. You are healing and you are allowed to feel. You are allowed to feel. Read some of the relief passages or soothing "I" statements to feel relief again.

If your sensitivities toward something come up or are triggered by someone or something then know that this is the area that requires work. It's asking for your focus and attention. It's saying, "look here. This needs more ease. It needs your breath. It needs your calm."

Breathe through the situation and remind yourself that it's okay for something to not be okay. It's okay for your parent to be upset; it's okay for your boss to be angry. Everyone is responsible for their feelings and your only work is your own. You are working on your feelings and your experience. Remove that responsibility you've placed on yourself. Your only job is to breathe into your body and into your experience.

If you take on other people's feelings and experiences too you will create disorders within yourself. You are one self and when you split that one self for others you create mental fragmentation and dysfunction. Bring yourself into yourself. Become whole as yourself.

Other people's feelings do not exist in you. Other people's experiences are not experienced in you. Don't think for them. Don't become them. You can't fix or heal them by doing that. You can't fix or heal yourself by doing that either.

Children who grow up with nervous system dysregulation due to early abuse become deeply empathetic and often times "feel" as other people feel. This will present itself during the contraction period. You will feel your own expansion and calm and then get pulled into others' anger or sadness. When you notice this happening, practice the mindfulness awareness in your body. Take deep breaths and notice where it's showing up. Remind yourself that you don't have to take on other people's feelings. It doesn't help them or you. It doesn't benefit anyone. All it does is rob you of your peace. You can help others through your stability much more effectively than you ever can through your chaos or dysregulation.

You don't have to mirror their feelings or behavior. You don't have to merge your energies or take on their characteristics. You don't have to attach to anyone else. Bring yourself back to yourself. Come back into your body. Come home to yourself. And breathe.

Deep Breathing:

Regardless of which negative feeling you feel, whether it's sadness, anger, or stress, you can immediately change the state of your body through focused deep breathing. You can use this exercise anytime for any reason.

Lie flat on your back on a yoga mat, a blanket, or your bed. Place your hands to your sides. Relax your body. Notice if any of your muscles are tense and relax them. Let your body go limp.

Breathe through your belly slowly. As you inhale, expand your belly out as much as you can, stretching out your belly muscles and hold it for four seconds. Then slowly exhale, releasing all the air. Do this about ten times. Keep your focus in your belly. Pay attention to how it expands and collapses. Feel the relief of the collapse, as you exhale out all of the air that once filled it.

Then raise your arms over your head and stretch out your body. Reach and stretch but don't hold your breath. Again, breathe into your belly, stretch it out, and exhale it down. Do this ten times with your arms over your head. Each time you do keep your focus in your belly, paying attention to the expansion and collapse. What sensations are coming up in your body? Does it feel good, relaxing, calming? You might feel your vagus nerve activating as you do this exercise.

After you finish doing that set, bring your arms back down to your sides and do the exercise again for ten breaths. You can do this exercise when you feel angry, stressed, or sad. It will put you in a more relaxed physical state and it only takes about 3 - 5 minutes to complete.

You might feel very relaxed so you shouldn't try to stand up fast because you might become dizzy. Continue lying on the mat after you're finished and breathe normally for a few breaths. Sit up slowly and then stand up.

You might feel some temperature changes as well with your body getting hot. You might feel some other part of your body burning up. You might feel tingling sensations in your belly, in your hands, in your head. It's all normal. As your body returns to a natural state of rest and your blood begins to circulate more easily, you'll feel the difference.

Breathing is a powerful tool. And while this exercise is an effective way to regulate your breathing, you won't be able to do it when you feel stressed in public or at work. The first thing you want to do in any kind of stressful environment is to become aware of when you hold your breath or when it becomes shallow.

This is common with people who have social anxiety. The holding of the breath is in anticipation of something negative occurring. You might also tighten the muscles in your gut as you hold your breath. A hyper-alert mind that expects stress will create tension and resistance in the body when it anticipates a negative experience.

Are you holding your breath? Is your breathing shallow? Consciously breathe when you notice you're holding it. Breathe as you walk. Breathe as you speak with others. Notice when you are not and release your breath.

The first place any kind of stress appears is in the breath. If you're holding it, if it's shallow or rapid, something is happening in your nervous system. Breathe to activate your parasympathetic nervous system and create calm in your body.

Explore Other Possibilities:

This exercise is simple and doesn't involve any physical work. It's an exercise for the mind. All you do is open yourself up to alternative possibilities in the moment. Just because something happened once before in a certain way doesn't guarantee that it will happen exactly like that again. Nothing in life repeats itself. Only emotion is repetitive. And what we really fear deep down is repeating the feelings underneath the event. We're afraid of feeling hopeless again, feeling powerless, feeling like we're not in control. That's where the real fear and stress is.

Just because you had a fight with your boss doesn't mean every time you two speak it's the same situation over and over again. It's a different situation each time full of different possibilities. Your mind just sees it as similar because it expects the same old response. It's reliving the past rather than seeing it as a new experience full of different possibilities.

So the first thing you do is get present to what the stressor is. Is that what's actually happening right now or a prediction of the future based on a past event? What is the current evidence that your fear will actually happen? Is that real evidence or an assumption based on what happened in the past? Is there another possibility or scenario that can happen?

Believing that your boss is going to reprimand you isn't any more valid than believing that he is going to reward you. They are both assumptions, both possibilities. Right now all that is happening is that you are speaking with your boss. There are several possibilities that can happen in that scenario.

Open your mind to other scenarios. Your brain is going to fight against that in the moment. Instead, it's going to say it's better to be safe than sorry. I'd rather be prepared than blindsided. This is the protective thinking you must overcome.

If you were bitten by a dog once, does that mean all dogs are going to bite you? No, but knowing that doesn't take away the pain from the past or the fear of it repeating in the future.

Out of the one hundred dogs you've come across, ninety-nine didn't bite you and one did. That's a dramatic difference. However, your mind is designed to only focus on the one that did bite you because it was a painful experience and it doesn't want to re-experience it. The brain is more likely to memorize painful experiences than positive ones. This is a part of our survival instincts.

Your brain is going to convince you that the only reason those other dogs didn't bite you is because your panic protected you. Because you did something against those dogs. You ran away or crossed the street. Your anxious actions protected you. That's the lie that stress tells you and that's the lie that keeps it alive. It disguises itself as useful protection and, generally speaking, it is. But not when it becomes a chronic disorder that affects your daily life.

So first you explore other possibilities to calm your mind so it's not too focused on the threat and then you reverse the thinking.

Are all dogs dangerous? If they were would so many people keep them as pets? Are all dogs going to bite you? Have all dogs bitten you? Is there a possibility that most of them are safe and loving?

Research some loving dogs, the ones who spend their days in hospitals helping the terminally ill feel love and support. Look at the guide dogs that help blind people get around safely. There are anxiety dogs, and epileptic guide dogs that help inform their owners when they're about to have a seizure so they can go lie down. There are dogs that detect cancer in petri dishes. Petting dogs has been proven to reduce high blood pressure because it activates the parasympathetic nervous system. They're helping the medical community in so many ways.

Yes there are also fight dogs, and guard dogs, and police dogs, and bomb-sniffing dogs used in war. Life is in no way all good or all bad. Neither is the thing you are afraid of or stressing about. There is a grounded mental approach to everything. It doesn't have to be black and white. It doesn't have to be pain or pleasure, good or bad, happy or sad. And that's really what stress and trauma does. It repaints your experiences in rigid scenarios where the only outcome you see is the traumatic event repeating itself. It's just not true. The only place it repeats itself is in your own mind.

Balance out your thinking through examples of wellness, through examples of positive outcomes. This is why we love stories about other people who overcame great obstacles. It inspires us and reminds us that not everything is a negative experience. We have the ability to turn them around. We may not have power over the past situation, but we have power over now. Which is a good thing because now is all there is.

All that matters is what you do now. It doesn't matter what you did or didn't do then. It doesn't matter how you handled it because the fact is that you are alive now, which means you handled it just fine. How did you survive the stressful event? How did you cope? If you're alive now, then that means you have some great traits that helped you survive.

You survived. You made it through. You're still here. That means something valuable. Don't take that away from yourself. So what if you didn't do things exactly the way you would do them now in hindsight? You did what helped you survive and you're still here, so clearly you did the right thing. Now, it's about forgiving yourself, it's about letting it go, it's about allowing yourself to move forward in healing. You can do that. You're ready to do that. So accept that there are alternative scenarios to stressful situations and that they don't have to be stressful. They can be, but they don't have to be. As long as you accept the possibility that they don't have to be, you're making progress.

Focus Beyond The Outcome:

When we feel stressed, it often narrows our focus to our stressors. We forget all of the wonderful people and circumstances in our lives that work well or make us happy.

Instead, we become consumed with the aspects that are currently stressing us out.

One simple technique that can help reduce stress is to focus beyond the outcome. Sit somewhere quiet and close your eyes. How would you feel if this stressor was resolved? Sit with those feelings for a moment. Visualize moving beyond the outcome, but don't think about the hows. It doesn't matter how it can happen, all that matters is that it has happened in your mind.

In your mind, you are jumping into the future where this outcome is in the past. You're done with it and have moved forward. Sit with those future feelings for a moment. You have now moved beyond the stressor. What does your life look like? How do you feel?

Allow your body to relax into the feeling of resolution. Once something has resolved, you're not as hung up on how it was resolved. You're just glad that you found a solution. Stay in that feeling of resolution and possibility. Open your eyes and keep feeling it.

Once your focus and perspective has changed, so will the stressor. You will begin to see it differently, and you might even discover a new way to approach it. Or better yet, it might not even feel like a stressor anymore. Repeat this a few times a week as needed and pay attention to how the situation changes for you.

Sometimes, focusing beyond the outcome shows us that it's not as bad as we think it is and it's entirely possible to be happy after the stressful event we fear is going to happen. Sometimes, that's enough to take away the tension and anxiety that comes with thinking about the event.

Soften Thoughts:

When you are in the middle of a stressful event, or even after a stressful event, if you can learn to soften your stressful thoughts, you can help your body return to regulation and ease much faster.

Let's say an event happens and it makes you upset. So you breathe into the upset and into your body. You make yourself present and you ground yourself. The next thing you would do is soften your thoughts around the event so that you don't become angry again after ten minutes. You don't want your interpretation of the event to retrigger the stress response so you have to do the mental work as well.

Let's say you have the thought: Nothing ever works out for me.

How would you soften that? By looking for examples that contradict it a little bit. Ask yourself, is that a true statement? Is it grounded in reality or emotion?

Some things work out for you. List a few of them. You graduated high school, or your kids are healthy, maybe you have a good job. Your spouse supports you. You have loving parents. Or you can pick smaller events, like the time you wanted a cup of coffee but had no cash and then you found a $5 bill on the ground. It doesn't have to be huge—just enough to add a little doubt. There are plenty of examples that will help you soften that thought.

"Nothing ever works out for me. Well, that's not true. Some things work out for me. If nothing worked out for me, then my life would be worse. "

Let's try another one.

"No one ever listens to me."

"Some people listen to me. In fact, most people do listen to me. They just don't do everything I say, which is fine because I don't control everyone. People are allowed to think and act for themselves, that doesn't mean they don't hear me or listen to what I have to say."

You can then make a list of all the times people listened to you or took your advice.

You can practice this exercise on paper first. Write down the negative thoughts as they show up during your day or after a stressful event. Then, sit down and soften them a little bit. Soften them enough where you can feel the relief of it, where you won't repeat the stressful thought regarding that issue without having your new negating thoughts follow immediately afterward. It will change your perspective of that belief, and you will never repeat it again because it will feel false.

Practice doing this on paper or on the notepad of your phone for a few weeks until you can do it in your mind automatically.

Pick The Thought That Feels Better in Your Body:

This exercise is similar to the one that came before it, but it's a bit different. As you have a thought that triggers resistance or tension, you immediately ask yourself, which thought feels better? And you adjust the thought a little bit until you find the relief feeling.

"I'm never gonna make it on time" or "I'm gonna try my best to make it on time." Which one feels more relieving? "I hate this job" or "This job has some positive aspects that I like"?

Which one feels better "I don't have enough money" or "I have enough money for some things"?

With this exercise, you're not trying to find the absolute truth because both thoughts might be true. The question is, which one *feels* better? Which one offers you relief? Which one is less likely to create stress and therefore make you sick in the long run? Which one is less problematic?

The purpose of this exercise is to get you into the habit of soothing yourself and creating ease in your mind. Once you stop triggering the stressful response through the habit of negative thought, you'll be in a better position to create better circumstances for yourself.

This exercise isn't about being blind to your reality. It's about finding the aspects of your reality that aren't as bad. It's about inspiring yourself into purposeful action. It's about allowing the joy to return to your life, regardless of your circumstances.

Once you shift your focus there and begin to feel better, your actions will improve. Your life will improve. Your joy will return. You deserve that.

Flip Negative Beliefs:

As you become open to alternative possibilities to stress, as you pick better feeling thoughts, then you can learn to flip your negative beliefs. It might take more practice because beliefs are a bit more difficult to change. We might not even realize we have them.

Take some time and sit down with a piece of paper. Write the negative beliefs you hold about yourself. Try to find as many as you can. "I can't trust anyone." "People always hurt me." "I'm not safe."

First, I would recommend going through the list and doing the body mindfulness exercise with each one of those beliefs to see if you can release them from your body so they don't return as sensations. Then, flip them in your mind so they don't return as thoughts.

You flip a belief by first creating doubt within it and then slowly turn it around. Let's try it with a few negative beliefs:

"I will always be stressed."

"There are people who have overcome trauma. There are people who have bounced back from the worst scenarios possible. It doesn't have to last forever or even until the end of my life. Traumas can be healed. Stress can dissipate. I'm committed to healing. I've already taken steps by reading this book, so there's no reason for me to always be stressed."

"I'm not safe."

"I've been safe most of my life. There were a few instances where it felt like I wasn't safe, but I'm alive now, which means I survived. I'm safe in this moment, and that means something. I'm a survivor and will always find safety in some way, shape, or form."

"No one loves me."

"That's not true. Plenty of people love me. They love me in their own way. Maybe they don't love me the way I expect or show it the way I'm used to, but that doesn't mean they don't love me. People show love differently. I show love differently from how others expect; does that mean I don't love them? Of course not."

"I can't trust anyone."

"There are many people I've trusted with important tasks and they have come through for me. I trust my partner to protect our children. I trust that my children's teachers will teach them. I trust that the garbage trucks will pick up the garbage. I trust that the grocery store will have food. I trust that if I truly needed help, I would be able to find it. There are many things in my life that I trust, and they run smoothly."

Once you create a little bit of doubt and write statements to turn it around, you then have to begin noticing the opposite of the belief in your environment. Make it a habit to acknowledge the new belief. You've been collecting evidence for the old one for years. That's how it strengthened. Now, you need new evidence.

When you are sitting with friends, having coffee, or watching TV, say to yourself, "I'm safe now. I can be safe. " When you are breathing deep or doing yoga and you feel good in your body, say to yourself, "I'm feeling better now. I'm in the process of healing." As you trust someone with a task and they come through, say to yourself, "I trusted this person with the task." As you do things that are the opposite of the negative belief, acknowledge them. This will focus your brain more and more on your new beliefs. "I am safe. I am healing. I am strong."

Instead of focusing on your fear or your stressor, your mind will begin focusing on finding evidence for your new belief. Right now, it's searching your environment for the old beliefs. So as you do your deep breathing, as you work through your emotions, begin shifting your attention to what is working, what is healing, what is safe. Show yourself it's all working out for you. Feel your relief. Trust it.

I have shared over 100 activities and steps for empowerment and managing your mind in my book, *The Empowered Self*. It also comes with a workbook, where you can answer questions, flip negative thoughts, and practice writing more positive ones. It's a book I recommend to people who would like to raise their self-esteem, practice self-compassion, and become more empowered. If you would like more exercises like this one, consider using that book to work on building stronger mental habits. It's strictly a brain-to-body book and will help you create better thinking patterns.

Self-Compassion:

The final exercise for this book is self-compassion. Nothing happens without that. If you continue to abuse yourself, run yourself down, and hurt yourself, you will never find relief or release. Sometimes, it's going to be easy; sometimes, it's going to be hard. You're going to have days where you feel good about your progress, and you're going to have days where you feel impatient and frustrated with yourself.

Finding balance mentally and emotionally works in a similar way. You take two steps forward and one step back.

Then, you take three steps forward and one step back. Maybe you take five steps forward and two steps back. But either way, wherever you are now in your step back, it's still forward from where you were a year ago. You can't un-experience, you can't un-grow, you can't un-expand. If you're doing the work, it's working. Just because you feel a familiar emotion doesn't mean you're back to square one. Depression is a familiar feeling. Anxiety is a familiar feeling. Cravings are familiar. But it's not the same because you're not the same.

Give yourself credit for how far you've come. It doesn't matter if you still feel what you felt before. It's going to happen. Emotions recycle. Growth is not a straight line; it's a spiral. You're going to come back around to the same things, but you'll be viewing them from a higher perspective.

So don't shame yourself, don't attack yourself, don't discourage yourself. You are exactly where you need to be right now in your growth. It's not wrong; you're not running late. You're not off course; nothing is ruined. Healing is a messy process. The wound doesn't disappear overnight. There's oozing and bruising and hurting, and you just have to stick with it.

As long as you stick with a well-rounded approach to balance and cover the five major areas, you will see great progress. If you want to begin in one area and then slowly incorporate the others, that's fine too. It's not a competition, and there is no finish line. We are always going to have something to heal. Some event at some time is going to bring up a past pain or issue. You will need to heal and release that, as well.

The only difference will be that you'll be regulated, feeling more ease, and much more prepared for future stressors and healing.

A well-rounded approach to healing covers five major areas: physical, mental, emotional, social, and spiritual.

The physical involves better sleep, better diet, supplements, water, and exercise. All of these factors will support your body, nervous system regulation, and your brain. It will lead to better functioning overall.

The mental involves working on not believing your own negative thoughts, removing the charge from stressful stories, and stress management techniques for current experiences.

The emotional involves allowing your emotions, easing them through mindfulness, and calming yourself consciously. And if need be, talking with a therapist.

The social involves deepening connections with others. Doing fun social activities, the kind that will keep you in the present moment. Traveling, exploring, and meeting new people. Get involved in your community. Reach out to a support group for trauma survivors—join AA (Alcoholics Anonymous) or NA (Narcotics Anonymous), join a church group. Do something that involves interacting in a deeper way with others.

The spiritual involves being purposeful in life. It's not so much about God, but it can be if you want it to be. This will be unique to you and what moves you. Where is your passion? Do something important, volunteer, help others, donate your time and energy to a cause bigger than yourself. Get out of your own suffering by helping to relieve the suffering of others. Do something that goes beyond yourself.

You don't have to do all of that at once because you will overwhelm yourself. Take it one step at a time, one activity at a time, one social event at a time. Don't overschedule yourself and trigger your protective need to isolate. Don't push yourself too hard. Step a little bit outside of your comfort zone each time. Do one small thing at a time, or do it in small degrees. Gradually increase the time and energy spent on it as you go along.

When you approach your healing through all of these areas, you will feel the difference in your mind, body, and life. Will negative feelings come up? Will stressful events happen? Of course they will. But you will be capable of handling them in such a way that doesn't physically or mentally hurt you.

You will be resilient. You will trust yourself. You will feel empowered and confident. The more you heal, the better you're going to feel about yourself. Not just because your mind and body will feel better, but because your direct actions created the healing. That feeling of control, the purposefulness of the actions, and the positive results will encourage you further.

You are going to be well. You're going to feel better than you've ever felt before. You are on your way to a balanced and regulated mind and body. Take your time, do the work, and you will see results.

In Conclusion:

Stress is nothing more than the uneasiness of the mind and body. Once you relearn ease, you can return to a state of healing, balance, and peace. Let the feeling of relief be your guide. Let it be your internal GPS that tells you you're on the right path.

Feelings are important to the human experience. Human beings were feeling beings long before we were thinking beings. According to neuroscientists who study the evolutionary development of the brain, emotions evolved first long before our ability to think and judge. They are a deep fundamental part of our biology. They are no less important, physiologically speaking, than developing ears, eyes, or hands.

We are feeling beings, and when we shame ourselves for feeling, when we numb ourselves or shut down, then we disable an important aspect of ourselves. When we deny our emotions, its as damaging as denying our feelings of hunger or thirst. All feelings are valid and important to our survival, to our wellbeing, and to our thriving.

Your emotions are the communication method between your mind and body. When there is a balanced connection, then there is harmony within the body and mind. When the connection is disrupted, numbed, resisted, shamed or repressed, then we become disoriented, off-balance, unwell, and uneasy.

We drift through life without a compass or guide, unsure of who we are or what we're doing. Life becomes emptier, and our relationships begin to suffer. We become more sensitive to stress and anger.

If we are not cultivating the connection within ourselves, then we can't truly connect to anything else. And if we can't connect, if we can't feel anything positive, then we merely exist in our lives. We become emotional zombies who can't feel fulfilled, satisfied, or happy. We move through life feeling frustrated, stressed, and easily angered.

It's important that we allow ourselves to feel what we feel. This is crucial to allowing more relief in our lives. Stress often gets repressed, shamed, or leads to self-abuse. If we allow our emotions more, then we minimize our stressful experiences. Then, we begin the healing process.

Wherever you are now, it's a good place to begin. Even if all you do is read and reread the relief passages over and over again, that's a good place to be. Begin the exercises when you feel it's the right time. Start where you start and take a rest when you need it. There is no pressure, no commitment, no struggle with this book. It's all about ease. It's all about relief.

You have permission to not finish it. You have permission to skip exercises. You have permission to do whatever you need to do with this book. Read it if it feels good, do it if it feels good, and ignore everything else. All that matters is that you feel relief, however small it may be in the beginning. It's not a competition, so it doesn't matter. There's no winning or losing, only relief.

I hope that you learn to be kind to yourself on this journey, and I hope that you allow yourself to work through your feelings and come out stronger and wiser than ever before. I hope that you improve your relationships and create more moments of peace and happiness.

I hope you find your joy again. I hope you reach that deep peace within yourself. You deserve it. You deserve to be well, you deserve to be happy, you deserve to be in balance. You deserve the best of this life. Believe it.

Resources and Studies

Theories:

Stephen Porges – The Polyvagal Theory
Porges, Stephen W. (2011). *The Polyvagal Theory: Neurophysiologial foundations of emotions, attachment, communication, and self-regulation.* New York: W. W. Norton & Company.

Dr. Peter Levine – Somatic Experiencing®
Levine, Peter A (2010). *In an Unspoken Voice: How the Body Releases Trauma and Restores Goodness.* Berkeley, CA: North Atlantic Books.

Eugene Gendlin – Focusing
Gendlin, Eugene T (1996). *Focusing-oriented psychotherapy: a manual of the experiential method.* New York: Guilford Press.

Special thanks to Jerry, Esther, and Abraham Hicks for offering relief and ease when I needed it the most. Your work was instrumental in helping me understand why a book of relief was essential to healing and progress.

Exercise Studies:

Relief Exercise: Breathe deeply: *Cardiovascular and Respiratory Effect of Yogic Slow Breathing in the Yoga Beginner: What Is the Best Approach?*
Department of Neuroscience, Roehampton University, London, United Kingdom
https://www.hindawi.com/journals/ecam/2013/743504/

Relief Exercise: Tense and release: *How to Perform Progressive Muscle Relaxation*
http://www.wikihow.com/Perform-Progressive-Muscle-Relaxation

Relief Exercise: Laugh: *The Effect of Mirthful Laughter on the Human Cardiovascular System.*
Dept of Medicine, Division of Cardiology University of Maryland Medical Center Baltimore, MD, United States
https://www.ncbi.nlm.nih.gov/pmc/articles/PMC2814549/

The effect of humor on short-term memory in older adults: a new component for whole-person wellness.
https://www.ncbi.nlm.nih.gov/pubmed/24682001

Relief Exercise: Listen to calming music: *Releasing Stress Through the Power of Music*
University of Nevada, Reno, NV, United States
http://www.unr.edu/counseling/virtual-relaxation-room/releasing-stress-through-the-power-of-music

A Dose of Music for Pain Relief
http://www.brainfacts.org/sensing-thinking-behaving/senses-and-perception/articles/2013/a-dose-of-music-for-pain-relief/

Relief Exercise: Float: *Eliciting the Relaxation Response With the Help of Flotation*
Departments of Psychology and Health & Caring Sciences, Karlstad University, Sweden
http://justfloat.com/wp-content/uploads/2016/03/Eliciting-the-Relaxation-Response-With-the-REST.pdf

Float hopes: The strange new science of floating.
http://time.com/floating/

Relief Exercise: Notice life more: *Effects of Mindfulness on Psychological Health: A Review of Empirical Studies*
Department of Psychiatry and Behavioral Sciences, Duke University Medical Center, Durham, NC, United States
https://www.ncbi.nlm.nih.gov/pmc/articles/PMC3679190/

Relief Exercise: Chant: *Neurohemodynamic correlates of 'OM' chanting: A pilot functional magnetic resonance imaging study*
Department of Psychiatry, Advanced Center for Yoga, National Institute of Mental Health and Neurosciences, Bangalore, India
https://www.ncbi.nlm.nih.gov/pmc/articles/PMC3099099/

Relief Exercise: Watch fish swim: *Marine Biota and Psychological Well-Being: A Preliminary Examination of Dose–Response Effects in an Aquarium Setting*
National Marine Aquarium, Plymouth, United Kingdom
http://eab.sagepub.com/content/early/2015/07/27/00139165155
97512.abstract

Relief Exercise: Dance: *Dancing and the brain.*
Department of Neurobiology, Harvard Medical School, Cambridge, MA, United States
http://neuro.hms.harvard.edu/harvard-mahoney-neuroscience-institute/brain-newsletter/and-brain-series/dancing-and-brain

Relief Exercise: Sing: *Music structure determines heart rate variability of singers.*
Center for Brain Repair and Rehabilitation, Institute of Neuroscience and Physiology, Sahlgrenska Academy, University of Gothenburg, Gothenburg, Sweden
https://www.ncbi.nlm.nih.gov/pmc/articles/PMC3705176/

Relief Exercise: Cut down on social media: *Seeing Everyone Else's Highlight Reels: How Facebook Usage is Linked to Depressive Symptoms*
http://guilfordjournals.com/doi/abs/10.1521/jscp.2014.33.8.701

New Study Links Facebook To Depression: But Now We Actually Understand Why
http://www.forbes.com/sites/alicegwalton/2015/04/08/new-study-links-facebook-to-depression-but-now-we-actually-understand-why/#7ad369042e65

Social media use associated with depression among US young adults
University of Pittsburgh Schools of the Health Sciences, Pittsburgh, PA, United States
https://www.sciencedaily.com/releases/2016/03/160322100401.htm

Relief Exercise: Strengthen social connections: *How positive emotions build physical health: perceived positive social connections account for the upward spiral between positive emotions and vagal tone.*
Department of Psychology, University of North Carolina at Chapel Hill, NC, United States

https://www.ncbi.nlm.nih.gov/pubmed/23649562

Relief Exercise: Increase physical touch: *The importance of touch in development.*
Brain Research Centre and Department of Psychology, University of British Columbia, Vancouver, British Columbia, Canada
https://www.ncbi.nlm.nih.gov/pmc/articles/PMC2865952/

The Experience of Touch: Research Points to a Critical Role.
http://www.nytimes.com/1988/02/02/science/the-experience-of-touch-research-points-to-a-critical-role.html?pagewanted=all

Relief Exercise: Practice walking meditation: *Exercise reorganizes the brain to be more resilient to stress.*
Department of Psychology, Princeton University, Princeton, NJ, United States
https://www.princeton.edu/main/news/archive/S37/28/70Q72/index.xml?section=science

Meditation experience is associated with differences in default mode network activity and connectivity.
Department of Psychiatry, Yale University School of Medicine, New Haven, CT, United States

http://www.pnas.org/content/108/50/20254.short

Relief Exercise: Stay curious: *The psychology and
neuroscience of curiosity*
Department of Brain and Cognitive Sciences and Center for
Visual Science, University of Rochester, Rochester, NY,
United States
https://www.ncbi.nlm.nih.gov/pmc/articles/PMC4635443/

Relief Exercise: Spend time in nature: *Nature experience
reduces rumination and subgenual prefrontal cortex activation*
Emmett Interdisciplinary Program in Environment and
Resources, Stanford University, Stanford, CA, United States
http://www.pnas.org/content/112/28/8567.abstract?sid=2c8fb2
36-95aa-4b2f-9b56-768a6960ed47

Relief Exercise: Practice gratitude: *In Praise of Gratitude:
Expressing thanks may be one of the simplest ways to feel
better.*
Harvard Health Publications, Harvard Medical School.
Cambridge, MA, United States
http://www.health.harvard.edu/newsletter_article/in-praise-of-
gratitude

<u>Relief Exercise: Meditate</u>: *Eight weeks to a better brain: Meditation study shows changes associated with awareness, stress.*

University of Massachusetts Center for Mindfulness, MA, United States

http://news.harvard.edu/gazette/story/2011/01/eight-weeks-to-a-better-brain/

Forever Young(er): potential age-defying effects of long-term meditation on gray matter atrophy.

Department of Neurology, School of Medicine, University of California, Los Angeles, Los Angeles, CA, United States

http://journal.frontiersin.org/article/10.3389/fpsyg.2014.01551/full

<u>Relief Exercise: Do some yoga</u>: *Sudarshan Kriya yogic breathing in the treatment of stress, anxiety, and depression: part I-neurophysiologic model.*

Columbia College of Physicians and Surgeons, New York, NY, United States

https://www.ncbi.nlm.nih.gov/pubmed/15750381

Effects of Yoga Versus Walking on Mood, Anxiety, and Brain GABA Levels: A Randomized Controlled MRS Study

Division of Psychiatry, Boston University School of Medicine, Boston, MA, United States
https://www.ncbi.nlm.nih.gov/pmc/articles/PMC3111147/

Relief Exercise: Do something physical: *Vagal nerve regulation is essential for the increase in gastric motility in response to mild exercise.*
Department of Physical Medicine and Rehabilitation, Tohoku University, Sendai, Japan
https://www.ncbi.nlm.nih.gov/pubmed/20948179

Relief Exercise: Run: *Effects of Running on Chronic Diseases and Cardiovascular and All-Cause Mortality*
Mayo Foundation for Medical Education and Research
http://www.mayoclinicproceedings.org/article/%20S0025-6196(15)00621-7/fulltext

Experts: Surprisingly Little Running Extends Lifespan: New report summarizes best research on running and health.
http://www.runnersworld.com/health/experts-surprisingly-little-running-extends-lifespan

Relief Exercise: Aromatherapy: *Aromatherapy: What is it?*
University of Maryland Medical Center, Maryland, United States

http://umm.edu/health/medical/altmed/treatment/aromatherapy

Relief Exercise: Get creative: *The Connection Between Art, Healing, and Public Health: A Review of Current Literature*
Department of Health Policy and Management, Harvard School of Public Health, Cambridge, MA, United States
https://www.ncbi.nlm.nih.gov/pmc/articles/PMC2804629/#__ffn_sectitle

Relief Exercise: Play with a pet. *Pets: Good for Your Health?*
http://www.newsweek.com/id/91445

Psychosocial and Psychophysiological Effects of Human-Animal Interactions: The Possible Role of Oxytocin
Department of Special Education, Institut für Sonderpädagogische Entwicklungsförderung und Rehabilitation, University of Rostock, Rostock, Germany
https://www.ncbi.nlm.nih.gov/pmc/articles/PMC3408111/

Relief Exercise: Journal: *Writing to heal: By helping people manage and learn from negative experiences, writing strengthens their immune systems as well as their minds.*
American Psychological Association
http://www.apa.org/monitor/jun02/writing.aspx

Relief Exercise: Hug more: *Does Hugging Provide Stress-Buffering Social Support? A Study of Susceptibility to Upper Respiratory Infection and Illness*

Department of Psychology, Carnegie Mellon University, Pittsburgh, PA, United States

http://www.psy.cmu.edu/~scohen/Does%20Hugging.pdf

Relief Exercise: Cold water: *Autonomic nervous function during whole-body cold exposure before and after cold acclimation.*

Institute of Health Sciences, University of Oulu, Oulu, Finland

https://www.ncbi.nlm.nih.gov/pubmed/18785356

Influence of cold water face immersion on post-exercise parasympathetic reactivation.

Laboratory of Exercise Physiology and Rehabilitation, Faculty of Sport Sciences, University of Picardie Amiens, France

http://link.springer.com/article/10.1007%2Fs00421-009-1253-9

Relief Exercise: Have an orgasm: *10 Surprising Health Benefits of Sex: The perks of sex extend well beyond the bedroom.*

http://www.webmd.com/sex-relationships/guide/sex-and-health

Sexual activity, erectile dysfunction, and incident cardiovascular events.
New England Research Institutes, Watertown, MA, United States
https://www.ncbi.nlm.nih.gov/pubmed/20102917

The Multiple Links Between Sex and Stress: Sex as a Stress Management Technique? Yes!
https://www.verywell.com/sex-as-a-stress-management-technique-3144601

Made in the USA
San Bernardino, CA
27 July 2018